Where My Ink Comes From

In this world, you will have trouble. But take heart! I have overcome the world.
                              John 16:33

For my son

Where My Ink Comes From

Sunday, January 13, 2008
Dear Diary,

    I love the smell of new paper in a journal. I go through one faster than I go through Wal*Mart sweaters. And it's not enough to have just a new journal that I like. I have to look at the entire section of stationery about a hundred times before I find the right one. And if I don't find one that I absolutely fall in love with, I go to a different store. This one has a leather cover with a buckle. I like the classy stuff.

    My dad wants to go to the music store today and get some new guitar strings. I keep trying to tell him that it's not open on Sundays, and to wait until after school tomorrow. I need to get a metronome. The one on my keyboard isn't cutting it. It's doing the opposite, and getting me off of my beat. I've an audition for Governors School for the Arts in March, and I'm so nervous. I auditioned last year and I was rejected. I promised myself I would get in this year, and I've been trying really hard to get ready for it.. I'm devoting ALL my free time to the piece I chose, and I've even stayed home from school a few days to practice. At school, I go into the Band room everyday during lunch to work on it. Mr. Jones, my Band director, is supposed to help me with it, but he hasn't really had the time.

    I'm so scared. I've wanted to get into GSA for so long, I don't know what I'll do if I don't. I decided a long time ago that if GSA wouldn't accept me, nobody would. So if I don't get in, I'm quitting music after this year. Between you and me, I'm not too sure it's what I want to do, anyway. Don't get me wrong, though. I love playing, and I love writing music even more. If I can't do my music in heaven, I don't want to go. But as a career, I just don't think I can do what Mr. Jones does everyday. Let's face it; he has to take a lot of crap from people who don't care about being there. Teaching music sounds wonderful, but I don't think I can do it. I've wanted to teach since middle school when I came to the high school to play in the Pep Band, but here in my junior year, now that it's time to start giving careers serious consideration, I'm not sure if I want to allocate my life to it. I wanted to come back here and teach at Green County High, but it might be a long shot, considering my poor attendance record. They remember these things, I'm sure...

    Actually, when I got rejected last year, GSA recommended me to the Youth Theater Conservatory. I went there and met a lot of new people. Riley, Jordan, Lauren, Brooke, Jason, and I were always together. I miss them a lot. I got to meet a lot of famous people, too; Sue Grafton, Stuart Kaminsky, William Link, George Keetz, among others. I guess if I don't get in, I can always go back there this summer. Maybe some of my friends from last year would be there. But it just wouldn't be the same, what with all the time I've put into GSA. I'm auditioning for drama as well as music, and I would be pleased to get in for that discipline. That being said, even though I love drama, I began with my music. I want to end my high school career on the same note. ...No pun intended...

    My wrists are hurting again. I'm probably just over-practicing. Maybe I'll ask Mr. Jones tomorrow about it.

                                                  Jessie

<u>Monday, January 14, 2008</u>
Dear Diary,

    Of course, we got into it again. My family is always arguing over something or another, and it's almost never about money, as so many of Dr. Phil's guests tend to choose as a topic of interest. Today, it was about my dad. His heart has been skipping beats, and what he says feels like 'flopping,' and he won't go to the doctor. I told him I would give him the $40 for the office visit if he would just go. He said he didn't want to, that he would be okay. And then he laughed in my face and said, "How much do you think a doctor charges? And how would I pay for the tests he'd want to run?" I reminded him that we couldn't afford a funeral either, and I'd rather have a hospital bill than have to pay for a casket. Needless to say, I didn't get my metronome today, but that's the least of my worries.

The problem is, after he had his heart attack and open-heart surgery last August, they took his medical card. I'm still not sure who 'they' are… but anyway, it's gone. And he doesn't have the money to go to the doctor. He already has to pay for some things that his insurance didn't go back and cover for him, like when we had to call the ambulance, part of his hospital stay, etc. Right now, he has to buy only a few pills at a time, or just whatever he can afford. He says he just wants to quit buying them and let whatever happens happen. He's stupid! He acts like he doesn't even care about living anymore. I don't have room to talk, though.

I don't want him to die. I'll lose my mind. I actually hope that when the time comes, I'll die first. I blame myself for his heart attack and having to have surgery, anyway. When I'm crying and he has to sit on the bed with me to make sure I don't try to kill myself again, look me in the eye and tell me diet caused it. Although, I can't imagine my brother helped, either. Between him and Mamaw, my dad has been known to call this place the house of hell. That's a big thing for my religious, never-swear Baptist father. I think I did the most, but they didn't help. It's amazing; my grandmother gets sick with age, so after my parents divorce, my dad takes my brother and I, and we all go live with her to take care of her. He gives up his life to take care of her, yet she aids in making his life miserable with her constant disapproval over everything he does. He's not home enough, he works too much, he doesn't spend enough time with his kids… just choose a complaint. As far as my brother goes, he's twenty-something, and still lives at home. He dropped out of high school and his mental stability makes life horrible for the rest of us.

    A few years ago, I tried to kill myself. It was a fun time, really. I was playing slice-and-dice with a razor everyday, several times a day. I was eating next to nothing, sitting in my room with the lights all off and nothing but a candle for hours on end, and the only person I cared about, my boyfriend, I had been dragging through the mud with me, and I was scared to death he was going to break it off any day. So I downed a bottle of Zoloft that my brother had left over from a few years ago, which probably helped in my survival; it was pretty old. The paramedic didn't think I was going to make it, and I found out later that he had told my grandmother on the phone that I wouldn't live.

    I ended up in the hospital's Intensive Care Unit, where I had to lie my way out of going to a loony bin. I didn't have to go, but my Dad ended up paying the price. He had to watch my every move to make sure I didn't slit my wrist, or there would be nights when he had to sit with me just watching me cry to make sure I didn't blow my head off because of all the guns in the house. I stayed home the rest of the school year, so when I went back to high school my freshman year, my dad said, "One slip-up, and you'll just have to drop out or do whatever you have to do to get out of school." I wasn't sixteen yet, so I couldn't quit school if I did something wrong. I made it to April without falter, and then the fear that came with failing my science class led me to the bathroom with a razor. I was facing expulsion, but teachers defended me at the board meeting that would determine my fate, and I was allowed to go back.

    Stress causes heart attacks. And if having to worry about your daughter killing herself, or getting expelled from school for having a razor isn't stressful, I don't know what is.

    My dad has a girlfriend that just isn't my family's idea of what he needs, either. We've heard from various people that she's been on drugs, sleeps around, and my grandmother feels the need to remind him everyday. When he says he's going to Ann's house, it's like a horse being let loose at a racetrack. Mamaw doesn't miss a beat in giving him a hard time, saying things like, "Go screw around over there some," or, "We don't have work to do here, or anything." And she gets on the phone and tells people I cry for him when he leaves, that I wish he would leave her alone.

    Truth? I don't care who he's with. I don't like her, but it's not because I believe all the garbage Mamaw claims she's heard. It's because I don't think she really loves him at all, and I think he needs to move on. So I guess we all played a part in my dad's heart attack, but I'm the biggest blame of them all.

Jessie

Friday, January 18, 2008
Dear Diary,

    I feel myself sliding back into one of my slumps. I hate when I get this way. I usually end up in a dark corner for weeks on end with a razor and fighting the urge to kill myself. I'm always depressed about something; I just have a hard time hiding it after a while. I guess with the audition coming up, Pep Band season in full swing, and knowing perfectly well there's something wrong with my wrists, I'm getting somewhat stressed.

    Maybe I just get to a point where I need some reassurance is all. But it's starting to show. I got in a fight with Taylor Wednesday. She started griping about how Christians think they're better than everyone else. At which point, I was like, "Yes, Blair just acts like she's so much higher up on the food chain than us. And yes, those were my exact words. Christians are the best people." You want to know what I really said? I wasn't even talking to her, but I said, "I don't know how you can be saved, go out and do something like set a bomb off in a daycare, and still go to heaven." And Taylor went off about how she didn't want to hear about it, that Christians were self-centered morons. So I just picked up my lunch tray and left. I wasn't going to waste my energy arguing with her ignorance.

    Taylor has always been that way. We can argue over just about anything, but only because she's so provincial to new ideas. I can't have a conversation religion-based anywhere around her, because she claims to be an atheist. I didn't bother reminding her of all the times she led hour-long conversations over how cool Egyptian gods are (when she said she believed in them in middle school). As for Blair, she plays saxophone in the Band. She's always my example, she's so perfect. She's a Christian, and it shows. I admire her. Actually, I'm jealous of her a little bit. She just seems so happy all the time, and I always wonder if her life is really that wonderful, or if God is really that wonderful.

    I'll be okay. Times like these, I usually end up writing all the time, and it seems to help somewhat. I stick to my notebook at school, and to you at home. And if nothing else, when I snap out of it, I come out with some good songs from my trip down. It's not like I have any friends to be around. I try to ignore Taylor as much as possible, because of all the fighting. My best friend has always been you, a journal, and you've always been good to me. We never disagree.

                                                            Jessie

<u>Monday, January 21, 2008</u>
Dear Diary,
    I hate nights like these. On this one, I sat out on the porch of the old cabin and cried. I haven't prayed in years. I do mean literally years. The last time was when Blair sat with me on the heater outside the Band room and started talking about God and that He still loved me. I went home that night and prayed, but

I don't think I believe it. There's too much wrong with my life for me to ever believe that God is here. If he loves me so much, why am I hurting so bad? I just don't understand. Sorry, Blair.

    I had been in my room upstairs practicing my stupid audition piece. And my wrists started hurting so bad, I couldn't stand it. I had been practicing since nine that morning with no break, and it was almost seven o' clock. I had even stayed home from school to practice. I still couldn't get this stupid 32nd-note run right on a part of the music, and I finally broke. I threw my Flute on the bed, grabbed my razor from off the dresser, started tearing at my arm, and I kept saying, "I quit. I don't care. I quit." And after a while, I just kept pressing harder on the blade, hoping I'd accidentally hit a vein. That's when I stopped. I scared myself. Most of the cuts I had would need stitches that I would never get, they were so deep. I fell into my chair, and just started praying.

    I didn't ask for this. Nothing in my life has worked out. I'm too young for everything I've tried to have failed. I can't keep anyone around; nobody wants to have anything to do with me. Nobody understands, or even cares, for that matter. At the last basketball game my school had when the Band played, someone came in and said that Mr. Jones wanted us back up in the stands to play, that our break was over. I stayed behind in the Band room to see if anyone would come back for me. No one ever did. I don't want to spend the rest of my life this way. I can't. I won't. Being forgotten is worse than death, and the world has obviously forgotten that I'm here.

    I've never been able to keep a friend. I eventually become too much for anyone to handle, so I just have to let them go. The last two friends I had ended up pulling a secret out of me that I've never told anyone. And you know what happened? They didn't believe me. That was Jamie and Nora. Nora was a senior my freshman year, so after she graduated, she didn't have much more to do with me. Jamie stuck around for a little while in her senior, but after she went off to college my sophomore year, she moved on and didn't keep contact. I gave up on her. Any friend I've had in the past, I've chased after and I've ended up losing, anyway. When it came time to tell Jamie goodbye, I let her go. Judging on past experiences, I didn't want to try to go after her, out of fear that I would be hurt again. When she left, I thought I was ready for it, but I still miss her horribly.

    Before that, it was my boyfriend during my little overdose. His name was Cameron. His mom didn't want him to have anything to do with me once she heard what happened, and being the perfect overachieving son he was, of course he was going to obey her. He ended up dumping me while I was still on the hospital bed.

    Mom... I was three months old when she ditched us. She swears up and down that my family just went through hell and high water to keep her away from us, and she was never a bad mother. I've heard stories from all sides. From my grandmother's side, I've been told that she was mean to me and my brother, that she beat us and neglected us when we had to go up to her house on the weekends. From her side, it was always some twisted version of what I had heard that made her out to be the good guy. Mamaw said she came home drunk from a Christmas party one time and threw me against the wall. Mom says she threw me to my Dad to get me out of the way of my aunt, that she was about to jump on her. That's just one example of many. And honestly, given my grandmother has gotten eccentric the last few years and has a funny way of making up and stretching stories, I believe her. But I'm not certain I want to know for sure who's telling the truth at times, or even if I care. It's obvious no one is telling the whole truth. That being the case, I say we just wipe the slate clean and go from here.

    She still comes around when she wants to. Growing up, I was lucky if I got to see her once a year. She would call a lot of the weekends she was supposed to come get me and my brother and tell us to get ready. What usually ended up happening was she would never show up. She always drove a different car, so each time we saw one coming or headlights shining, we would run to the window and hope that it was her. It never was. On the rare occasions that she did show up, it was late into the night, and she would have to wake us up to go. When I was twelve, she was gone completely. Three years later, she sent me a card that jumpstarted communication again. She told me she thought I hated her, and that was why she kept her distance. I spent a summer with her to give her a chance. She bought school clothes, got me a haircut and highlights, we went to museums and theme parks, all like she was trying to make up for lost time. She drives a truck now with her girlfriend. That was something else she told me while she was up there. She said, "I think you're cooler with my being gay than Eric would be, so let's not say anything to him now." I had heard the rumors from her dad who still came to visit us, so it wasn't surprising to me.

    Mom didn't want me, I have no friends, and my family doesn't care. I'm all alone. I prayed tonight that if God had anything planned for my life, if I had a purpose here besides proving that He makes mistakes, He'd better show me. Because I'm going to do this audition, and after that, I'm gone. GSA would give me something to look forward to, but if life is always going to be this way, I won't be a part of it.

Jessie

Thursday, January 31, 2008
Dear Diary,
    Everyone has a secret.

Jessie

Where My Ink Comes From

<u>Monday, February 4, 2008</u>
Dear Diary,

  I went to the doctor after school today. When I asked Jones this morning what he thought of my throbbing wrists, he told me it was just over-practice. Guess what? Tendonitis. I'm not supposed to play for six weeks, I have to take steroids to help repair the tendons, and wear these ugly braces for two weeks. I'm dreading tomorrow when I go back to school and get all the looks. No one at school has forgotten what happened freshman year, and the thought of me having an injury that isn't my doing is ridiculous to them. And even more, I really needed those steroids, the way I've been feeling lately. Jones told us a story once about how the doctor put him on steroids for a reason I forget now, but he said it made him crazy. I may die before this is over. I'll pop the pills and wear the braces, but I'm playing. Sorry. GSA is too important, and I'm not ready as it is.

  On the plus side, I just finished writing a narrative. I called it *Depression*. The format was inspired by another writer from my college English book who wrote about poverty. It's not actually about Depression as an illness, or anything like that. Most of the paragraphs begin with, "Depression is…" and fill in the blank; feeling mute, powerless, craving control, whatever else I said… It turned out really nice. Mandy wanted to read it. She's the other Flute, but she's not in class Band. We've been friends for a while, and I'm wondering how long it can last, considering she's leaving for college this fall. Anyway, I felt bad, but I told her no. My problem with writing is that too much of it ends up in notebooks and on computers to never be read, because I don't want people to enter into that part of my life. People know me just the way I am. Imagine taking your clothes off in public! That's the equivalency of what I would be doing by letting people read. I trust people to be understanding, I think. I just don't want to put the theory to the test and discover that I was wrong the hard

way.
        The secret last night… I'm not a virgin anymore. It wasn't pleasant, nor the fairytale first time I thought it would be.. I don't want to think about it, and as far as I'm concerned, nothing happened... Don't ask me...

Jessie

<u>Tuesday, February 5, 2008</u>
Dear Diary,
        I'm at the cabin again. I'm so glad my dad built this place. On nights when my family won't stop shouting, I come here to get away from it. But I shouldn't have to leave home to find peace to begin with. And Eric shouldn't be so egotistical. He kept screaming at our dad not to ever touch him with his nasty hands, and calling him a worthless, lazy bum, all because he brushed up against him in a small kitchen. I went off on him. "Yeah, mom didn't want us, and when he stepped up to raise us by himself, that made him a lazy bum! You're the deadweight!" Dad said to leave it alone, so I just left him. He won't fight for himself, but he doesn't want anyone else to fight for him, and he just takes his crap all the time.
        My brother is crazy. I don't mean the kind of crazy that he's weird around the edges, or stuffs tots in his pocket. I mean, he's really bad bipolar. He does stuff like this all the time. He threatens to beat us all up regularly when things don't go his way, beats and throws our two dogs around, and beats them again when they bite him. He runs through the house, doing and saying ridiculous things. Earlier today, he said he thought he had testicular cancer and wanted to be taken to the hospital. And he was SERIOUS! And he'll go from that directly into something like, "I'm going to go shoot zombies in my room," or, "I want to

join the National Guard." It's like his body can't keep up with his mind. Or maybe it's the other way around. He's insane. When he was little, he was unnaturally violent towards animals, and on video games. You'd be amazed at what he would do to a Barbie. Now, he's big enough to act out his fantasies, and that scares me.

Jessie

Wednesday, February 6, 2008
Dear Diary,

    I had to cut again today. Nothing happened in particular. Sometimes I make myself sick just thinking about different things. My audition is in less than a month, and Jones still hasn't set up a day to help me. I keep asking him, but I don't want to pester him excessively. Tell me... Is it possible to care about something too much? Maybe I'm putting too much on this whole audition. It's important to me, but does it really matter? And when I get in these little slumps, I start to remember the past, and it still hurts; people I've lost, things I've seen and been through... It's too much. I just want to forget it all.

Jessie

Monday, February 18, 2008
Dear Diary,

    I went to see Dr. John today. He wants to keep me on the steroids for another week. He did an x-ray, and I'm supposed to go to a physical therapist. My health insurance won't pay for it, though. We all have medical cards, and you don't get treatment on those things until you're basically on your deathbed. And then when you're declared terminal, they cut your insurance altogether.   I have to practice today, and I don't think I can take it. My wrists hurt so badly. He said if I didn't stop playing, I would probably end up having to have surgery.

Between all this, home, my teachers piling on the homework, the Band, and whatever else is going on in my head, I'm losing it. I'm cutting every night, bad cutting, and I still can't snap out of this slump I'm in. I can't even say I'm bipolar. I'm never happy, and that is only followed by intervals where life doesn't seem worth living. And death sounds so good right now. I had this dream last night – and I know it sounds weird – that I was dead. I was in the Band room playing my Flute, and Jones and Cameron were in the office just a few yards away from me. When they come out, I was trying to get their attention, and finally realized they couldn't see me.

You know what, though? I don't want to die. I really don't, but I don't see life ever being anything different from what it is now. I'm always going to feel this way, even if I do get out of this house. After the audition, I'll be able to tell by the judges' faces and questions if I'm in or not. If I don't get in for drama or music either one, then I don't have any talent worth hanging onto. If I can't get into GSA, I can't compete with anyone else. How can I make a career out of something I can't do? I don't do anything else but music. Even my writing is horrible. I don't have anybody, and I don't see how I'll ever make it to college. And with all the memories haunting me, it's just not worth it.

Jessie

Tuesday, February 19, 2008
Dear Diary,
	I hate this school, I hate the people in it, I hate the Band, the teachers, the students, everyone, everything, my classes… I hate it all. I miss when Nora and Jamie were here, and they didn't care about the things I had done in the past. They didn't hold anything against me. Even if that would come to change, I could at least pretend for the moment that it was always going to be that way. I was just too much of a burden for them. I don't want to be close to anyone, to keep from being hurt again. I don't want to hurt anyone else, either. Jamie proved that I'm good at that when she tried her best to help me. I think she left never knowing that I valued having her in my life, because my selfishness would never allow us to just be friends. But I'm so sick of being alone. I wish I could tell someone about the things I've kept secret so long. But no one would understand, or even want to hear it. I'm not telling anyone. I can't. I won't. It's no one's burden but mine, and I'll carry it alone. On nights like this when the flashbacks won't stop coming, and I keep reliving the memories, I'll just stick to my razor and put on a smile.
	I almost hope I don't get into GSA now. It'll all be over when I don't, and I'll never have to remember the memories again.
							Jessie

Thursday, February 21, 2008
Dear Diary,
	I get up the nerve to kill myself, and I don't even do it right. I took thirty Benadryl last night, wrote a letter to no one while I waited for them to kick in, and laid down in the bed. I ended up puking, passing out, and waking up to a huge mess. I guess I trashed my room. I'm just really sick and shaky today. I'm

sure to all the teachers, I look like I'm high. My pupils are huge. I feel funny all over. I probably need to go to the hospital, but they would just ship me off somewhere. My heart is jumping around all over the place. For several hours after, I couldn't even really think. I would have a thought, and lose it not even a second later. And the longer I tried to remember what it was, the more clues that left me. I guess this is what a drug addict feels like. I'm really sleepy. I hope nobody suspects anything, but nobody notices me any other time, so they shouldn't today.

    Diary, what happened to me? I was leaving school today, and I just got myself caught up in the loneliness of the day, the dread of seeing what a grim future holds, and the hurt from the weight of it all.

    Don't think badly of me. I'm not this way, really. It was just a really bad night, one that only goes to show I'm so stupid, I can't even kill myself right...

                                            Jessie

<u>Friday, February 22, 2008</u>
Dear Diary,

    I went to the doctor today and found out about my x-ray. He wanted to make sure there weren't any broken bones, but he's sure it's tendonitis. More steroids, more therapy, less playing. Auditions are almost a week away. He might as well have just told me not to breathe. Not going to happen, doc. He said, "I know you want to practice for this school. But I can't guarantee that you'll even be able to play if you keep this up. If you damage your wrists badly enough, you'll never play again." I told him that was okay, since this was the only way to prove whether or not I needed to pursue my music anymore. He just looked at me like I had grown four heads. "There are far worse things in life than not getting into the school of your dreams." Says who? The doctor who got into medical school and passed with flying colors?

    Mandy's been doing the same thing. She keeps saying, "You need to take a break. A day might make all the difference." She seems to think a day of rest before auditions will get my wrists back up to par, besides take my mind off things. And I think that I will just worry the whole day about all that lost practice time. She just doesn't understand. Then again, who does?

                                                                   Jessie

<u>Wednesday, February 27, 2008</u>
Dear Diary,

    I'm so scared. We all are. Jones has never just up and left us before. The principle, vice principle, and guidance counselor came in together to get him. They pulled him out of his office and took him into the hallway. Only Mr. Reynolds, the principle, came back in. Jones didn't even come back for his coat or bag. We might have passed it off as a family emergency, except that they were all so bent on keeping it hushed. They wouldn't even tell us if he was alright.

    Mr. Reynolds pulled the Band together before the pep rally to talk about the game that night. He wanted to know if we would be able to handle it by ourselves. That was a stupid question anyway, considering everyone knows Jones has always been able to trust us to run the show if he hasn't been able to be there for some reason. Several people asked where Jones was. Every time, we just heard, "You don't need to know that right now."

    I was so angry. We're all scared to death that something serious is wrong. And they're stupid! Don't they know he's going to tell us as soon as he gets back? If he comes back? I don't even want to think about that. We were supposed to play at the pep rally, and didn't. Instead, I sat by Mandy and griped at her about the whole situation. I was so upset. She finally said, "You're not the only one that's scared, and if he's in trouble, us getting upset over it is bound to make it worse." Maybe it upset me more than it should have. Or maybe I was the only one making it known.

After we left the gym, I went to find Mrs. Holly, my English teacher from freshman year. We talk all the time, and if there's anytime I need inside information, I get it from her. She said she didn't know anything about it, and didn't even know he was gone. It really surprised me that even the other teachers don't know. Maybe he really doesn't want us to find out what happened.

Please say he didn't do anything wrong. Tell me he's coming back.

Jessie

Thursday, February 28, 2008
Dear Diary,
How can I be so selfish? Mr. Jones is gone, and could be getting fired or worse, for all we know. And I'm worried about my stupid audition. I call my brother selfish, but I'm no better. I left school early today. I just can't stand being there with this mess going on. It's not him not being here that upsets me. It's not knowing whether to be angry, or scared, or worried… we don't know how to react. Blair's sister talked to him on the phone, and all we know is that he's okay. But what's going on? Even on the phone, we got the same you-don't-need-to-know-that-right-now response that Mr. Reynolds gave us. Why would he just leave us? There I go again. Selfish. He has bigger things to worry about. But you know, I think I'm just going to be selfish today.

I'm worried about the audition. Jones never even got a chance to help me. Period. I've done this piece by myself. I'm not going to get into GSA with my skills. I need him. And even more than this stupid audition, I was hoping maybe I could talk to him, that maybe he could say something to me that I hadn't thought of before. He has never led me wrong, and I've never regretted having listened to him about anything before. I don't want to die nearly as bad as I want the pain to stop, but I can't talk myself out of it.

I'll know Saturday after the audition whether or not I'll be in school Monday...

Jessie

Friday, February 29, 2008
Dear Diary,

Blair's sister called Jones again today. He's coming back Monday! I'm so relieved. We still don't know what happened. He said he would tell us about it during Band when he got back. Whatever happens Saturday, I may stick around long enough that I can find out what went on.

If I'm so happy about him coming back, why do I feel so numb?

My audition is tomorrow. I'm not ready. I've spent so much time on my music, I haven't even looked at my monologue. It's by Abigail from *The Crucible*. I don't even have it memorized. I don't know why I'm bothering with drama, anyway. The only reason I'm auditioning is because my teacher from the theatre academy I went to last summer thought I could get in. I know. Dumb, right? It's not even for me. So I'll crash-memorize tonight, and try to master my scales. I can't do anymore with my piece than I've already done. At this point, only a miracle will

help.
      Marissa is coming over today. She goes to another school now, and I miss her a lot. We used to be really good friends. I guess you could say we still are, but I never get to see her now. We would laugh at some of the dumbest things! Last year at my GSA audition, we saw a squirrel get hit by a truck on the road in front of the college where auditions were being held. And when it got hit, it squeaked! We were practically scream-laughing for the rest of the day. Marissa was laughing because it was funny; I was laughing because she had a laugh of gold. She's going to go with me to keep me sane, 'cause I'm going to be a nervous wreck. Besides being life or death for my music career, I'm trying to find a reason to hold on. If I can get in the school, I'll have something to look forward to. I don't right now. And that's a miserable existence.
Jessie

<u>Saturday, March 1, 2008</u>
Dear Diary,
      I should be practicing. This couldn't be a better time for me to be deathly ill. I hope it's not nerves. If it is, I'm going to puke all over the judges. I've been downing Pepto-Bismol since I woke up last night with a really bad stomachache, and I feel really nauseous. I think I've thrown up everything I've eaten in the last month. Every part of my body hurts. If this doesn't let up, I don't know how I'm going to make it through the audition. Just wait. I'll end up with the stomach flu, and have to miss a week of school to get over it, and I won't even make it to the audition site. I don't even want to think about that.
Jessie

Where My Ink Comes From

<u>Saturday, March 1, 2008</u>
Dear Diary,

  That's it. It's over. I had one of those auditions where everything that could have gone wrong did. And I do mean everything.

  First, the dress pants I counted on wearing, my only pair, don't fit anymore. That's odd, considering I wore them only a month ago for church, and they fit perfect. So I had to put on a black dress and put a dress shirt over that. Even the dress was tight. I'm fat enough, so I don't need to be gaining. Needless to say, that put me in a good mood the rest of the day. And the shoes I wanted to wear were falling apart, and I didn't have any other shoes to match the only dress outfit I had. I had a pair of pink heels that I threw in the car. I figured if something happened that my shoes broke, having a pair that doesn't match the rest of you is better than going into an audition barefoot.

  I also needed to take headshots of me to the audition to give to the judges. Marissa brought her camera, and we took the pictures. We had to take them to Walgreens and get them developed, and it took longer than what they thought. She had brought two cameras with her, and she grabbed the wrong one! So I didn't have my photos.

  She apologized profusely all the way to Murray. "Jessie, I'm so sorry! Really, I'm sorry. I didn't know."

  "It's alright." She wasn't going to listen. She kept apologizing, and I was getting too disheartened at how things were going to try and argue her into a calm.

  I thought it was over. Oh, but then God laughed, and decided on the walk to the fine arts center, I should snag my stockings on a fence post. And what's worse, I hadn't shaved my legs. So I had to either leave them on and look like white trash, or take them off and look like white trash. Not five seconds after that, my shoe split in half. No, the heel didn't break off. The shoe literately split in two pieces, right down the middle, and how I managed to do that is beyond me.

    I started crying right there. Marissa kept telling me to pull it together, that it would be okay. She wasn't the one putting her future on the line. I wanted to scream at her right there that this audition was determining my fate, but knew better than to do so. She ran back to the car and got my ugly pink shoes for me, I put them on and I rushed upstairs to take my stockings off and try to warm up. GSA said on their website they wanted you there 45 minutes early, but I got there just in time to get my Flute together and get my music out. Marissa was still feeling terrible because of the photos, and I was in no shape to try to convince her different, although I knew it wasn't her fault.

    I get to the hall outside the room where we audition, and wait in the line. The guy sitting there that took care of the auditions list was looking at me funny, and I couldn't figure out why. He gave me some tips for the judges, like look them in the eye, and give a firm handshake. And then he was like, "By the way, you've got something pink on your shirt. Better not let the judges see. If you don't look the part, they won't take you."

    How do I respond to that? I had to take some more Pepto-Bismol in the practice room, and I had spilled some on my WHITE shirt. He said he would switch me up so I could go try to get it off. So I was later getting into my audition so me and Marissa could go scrub my shirt for an hour. It still wouldn't come off. I was finally begging her to leave with me. "Let's just go home and forget it, Marissa. I'm tired, anyway." She kept pushing and shoving, and by the time I actually met with the judges, they could tell I was a nervous wreck. I'm sure they heard it in my playing.

    Jones said there are two good indications that you're accepted. First, you don't get cut off. If you get cut off, you can forget it. And second, if they ask a lot of questions, you're in. I got cut off, and they asked me one question. "Why do you want to go to GSA?"

"To better myself as a musician."

And that was it.

Come to think of it, that's exactly what happened at last year's audition when I failed. And I think I said it word for word, too.

The drama audition didn't even matter anymore. It went okay, considering I hadn't even done the monologue until I got in there. I had just memorized it. Actually, I think I had the best one out of the group audition. But it wasn't music, and it's not what I want to do with my life. Wanted.

I'm holding off until Monday. I want to see Jones to know he's okay and tell him how the audition went; but after that, I'm done. My music was the only shot I had of getting out of this place. And now, I've just proven to myself that I don't have what it takes to make it. I'd rather die than live the rest of my life this way.

Last night before I went to sleep, I wrote "GSA ACCEPTANCE" on my ceiling. I thought that would be the last thing I looked at and thought about when I went to sleep, the acceptance letter in my hand. So much for that idea.

Jessie

Monday, March 3, 2008
Dear Diary,

Jones was back at school today. And I can't remember the last time I hated anyone this much, short of my brother. Not Jones; Joshua, the punk kid that decided he was going to get our Band director reprimanded.

  This kid said something about Jones when he was on the bus going home one afternoon, and the bus driver felt the need to report it. I don't know all the details. I don't want to know them. And Jones didn't tell us exactly what was said. When he was explaining things to us, he didn't focus on what had happened. Instead, he reminded us that the reason he knew we would be okay was because he had taught us to stand on our own. He said, "I've taught you well enough that I don't need to stand next to you and hold your hand to know you know what you're doing."

  He was right. The only reason my audition piece sounded as good as it did was because he taught me. And his teaching is what has made me the musician I am today, even if I do consider myself mediocre from time to time. I didn't need his help, because he had already helped me all he could. I didn't need his lessons to prove that.

  Joshua. I hate him. The whole Band does now. He plays trombone in Pep Band, but he's never acted like he cares to be there. I don't think he'll be back now. And I'm so glad this is over.

Jessie

<u>Monday, March 3, 2008</u>
Dear Diary,
  I went to the store today and bought everything I needed. I have two bottles of aspirin, envelopes (so I'll have one for the letter I want to write), and a pregnancy test. I just walked through the aisle where they were, and realized aunt flo should have visited two weeks ago. I don't think I am. It's just what happened that one night, but you never get pregnant the first time. It's more for curiosity than anything, and I'm still going through with my plans.

I wrote my letter to everyone and put it in the back of this journal. I figure this is going to be the first thing they read, so they'll find it here. When I left school earlier, I said a subtle goodbye to everyone, and hoped that maybe they would see it in my eyes. But they have more important things to worry about than me, let's face it.

I'm taking this test out of strict curiosity. The results won't matter, especially considering the way it happened. I'll have to wait, because the test calls for the first bathroom run of the morning. But I don't have to go to school tomorrow. I don't know though, I always pictured myself dying on a Monday night. There's no significance to Monday, just that I think it's a pretty good day to die, since you won't have to go through the rest of the week. I'll just skip tomorrow and spend my last day at home. I have things I could be doing to wrap things up, anyway. I want to get my writings together so my family will have them, and get rid of other writings I don't want them to read.

I've toyed with this idea for years. I never thought I'd ever be this serious about it...

Jessie

Tuesday, March 4, 2008
Dear Diary,

I can't be pregnant! The test is wrong! I only paid a dollar for it. There's no way a test that cheap can be accurate! I didn't expect it to be positive. What do I do now? No worrying. It's false. It's a false result.

I told Mrs. Holly, anyway. I found her in the bathroom on monitor duty early this morning, first thing when I got to school, and asked if she could get away for a minute. "What's going on? Is it something bad?"

Bad? Only a little. "Yes. It's bad."

"I can't sneak away right now. Write it." She handed me a post-it note and a pen, and I wrote words that I never thought I'd be writing unless they were for some fantasy character in my notebook. Writing *I'm pregnant* seemed to make it sink in. This couldn't be right...

She folded up the paper. "I assumed something like that."

Wait a minute... You assumed that? Why? Do I come off as someone who would sleep around?! No, I can't be mad at her. And I'm not. Just scared. Scared.

I feel sick. Absolutely sick. Not morning sickness sick, but a timorous sick. What do I do? Do I go ahead and kill myself, knowing that I'm taking someone with me that doesn't get a say? I'd be about six weeks, right? It might not even be conscious, so it wouldn't matter. But then it doesn't even get a chance to live. It... what is it? A baby? A mass of cells? What? Surely not another human. I'm not supposed to be pregnant.

I told Mr. Jones, too. I regret doing that. I went into his office this morning, said I needed to talk to him, but I was afraid of what he would say. After I stood there silent and looking stupid for a few minutes, I finally said I think I might be pregnant. He wanted to know who the father is. I told him I couldn't tell him. I can't even write it down in here. It's too much to take in.

Jones said, "Go to the doctor, Jessie. The 'Error Proof Test' isn't error-proof." My grandmother goes to the doctor every Monday to get her blood checked for thickness, so I'll probably go next Monday. Does that mean I'm going to hang on until then? I may have to now. I don't want to. I would have to raise the baby at home, assuming my dad doesn't get so mad he kicks me out of the house. I don't think he would, but gosh, this is going to hurt him. And I can't even tell them that I didn't ask for this. Diary...

I didn't want kids. I didn't even want to get married. I was the one that while all the other girls were planning their weddings in kindergarten, I was off coloring, or drawing, and thinking how stupid they were. I couldn't name the father, much less marry him. It's not that I slept with a bunch of guys or anything. I know who the father is. But I just can't say who he is. I can't.

      God, listen to me. I'm not even pregnant. There's no way I could be. I feel stupid telling Jones and Holly now. Aunt flo is just late visiting, that's all. As for the positive pregnancy test, I'm sure it just happens from time to time, especially considering the test was so cheap.

      I'm not pregnant. I'm not. I promise myself that I'm not.

                                                  Jessie

Wednesday, March 5, 2008

Dear Diary,

      I'm still sick from the audition. I'm wondering if it was nerves, or just morning sickness. But now I'm scared. If I got into GSA, I wouldn't get to go. By the time the day came to leave for the school, I'd be as big as a house. Not that I'm not already fat, but still... No, I couldn't go. I've tried for two years to get into that place, only to have the events of one night take it away. Of course, I probably have bigger problems than that right now...

      But I'm not pregnant! It's the stomach flu, or something, and a cheap test. I'm not pregnant. I stayed home from school today, I was so sick, and I spent most of the afternoon rubbing my stomach and thinking about everything. I kept thinking how stupid I'm going to feel when I go to the doctor and find out I'm not pregnant. And I'm not. I'm not pregnant.

                                                  Jessie

Monday, March 10, 2008
Dear Diary,
  I went to the doctor today. I told Dr. John I thought I was pregnant. I got a blood test. A nurse said I could call tomorrow for the results.
  Jones assigned us to write our own score sheet for Band class...
  The Navy Band is playing tonight at Murray State University...
  This can't be happening...
Jessie

Tuesday, March 11, 2008
Dear Diary,
  Well, that's it. It's over. I'm pregnant. I'm really, really, really pregnant. I borrowed some girl's cell phone from my keyboarding class before it started and I went to go call the hospital. I told them my name, and that I was calling for my test results. I don't think I'll ever forget the woman saying it. "You ARE pregnant." She put emphasis on the 'are.' She connected me to the front desk of the hospital to get my follow-up instructions from Dr. John. I have to see him Monday.
  They're wrong. I know it.
  This is all so weird. I'm not the kind of girl that gets herself knocked up. I've seen girls in my school get pregnant, and they're all drug addicts, smokers, get into fights, and they spend more time home on suspension than they do in class. I'm not like

them. I play in the band! My grades aren't beautiful, but they're decent. I only tried smoking once when I was in middle school, and never had a desire to do it again. The most I've ever drank was tasting my Dad's homemade wine and ONE glass of Peach Arbor Mist at Thanksgiving last year that I didn't even sneak around to do because my mom gave it to me, and the most trouble I've ever gotten into was an after-school detention for being late for first block. I sit in the back of the class, I don't talk to anybody, I don't get in trouble, I never raise my hand, and no one feels the need to acknowledge me. I don't even really swear. I'm not the kind of girl who gets pregnant. People won't even believe I'm pregnant. I've never looked like I could be with anyone, by our school's social standards. I'm fat, I have black hair with brown roots that ALWAYS show no matter what I do, and obnoxious black-rimmed glasses. And I never seem to dress like anybody else; I wear long sleeves all year long because of my scars, and I can't stand makeup or excessive jewelry. And now I'm all alone and pregnant. People are going to wonder who was desperate enough to have sex with someone that looks like me.

    When I got back to class to give the girl back her phone, we had a substitute. I felt physically ill, and I was afraid she wouldn't let me leave. She did, and I just went to the bathroom and cried. I had a Bible in my backpack that I carry with me everywhere. I don't associate myself with God too much, since I never earned the right. I just opened to Psalms and started reading random chapters. It wasn't much of a comfort, though. It just reminded me that I'm so alone in this, even God isn't on my side.

    God, how can I be pregnant...?

Jessie

Where My Ink Comes From

<u>Thursday, March 13, 2008</u>
Dear Diary,
      I went shopping with Mary today. She used to date my dad and she was my grandfather's home health nurse before he died. She's just a friend a family friend now. Prom is coming up and she wanted to go look for a dress. We went to David's Bridal, and to a few consignment shops where they sold dresses. I found a lot that I liked, but I don't have a date, and I don't think I'm anyone's choice.
      We went to the Chinese restaurant to eat. She noticed that I was barely touching my food, and asked if I was sick. I haven't been able to eat very much at all lately. I haven't felt sick, really, but I can't bring myself to eat very much at all. I never feel hungry, and when I do eat, it doesn't take much for me to feel sick.
      Ironic that she would ask the question as a joke. "You're not pregnant, are you?"
      My stomach turned; not out of morning sickness, but at seeing the face she gave me when I didn't laugh with her. "You're not pregnant, are you?" She said it again with more concern and discretion the second time around.
      I nodded. I was pregnant. She said she wanted to help, and that she would raise it if I decided I couldn't do it. That would be the best decision for everybody, but my family would never let me. If I did that, all I'd hear for every Christmas and Thanksgiving and weekend I was home how horrible of a person I am, and how I'm just like my own mother. I'm either going to slit my wrist or be a mother.
      ...When they find out, anyway...
                                                         Jessie

Saturday, March 15, 2008
Dear Diary,

    Between eating next to nothing and waking up to go pee more than John McCain, you would think I'd never even have to say anything. You'd think my family could just figure it out on their own and spare me the shame of admitting that I got myself knocked up.

    I don't know what I'm going to do now. I still have the aspirin, and I wrote a letter to everyone. It's not to anyone in particular, just more or less why I'm doing this. Or rather, why I was. Does this mean I'm not going to do it? I still want to. I just don't think I could stand it if I ended up living and my baby didn't. No baby. What baby? I'm not even pregnant.

    They're wrong. I'm not pregnant. The hospital switched the tests, or something. There was some kind of mix-up. Or there's some other reason I'm getting a positive result. I'll look it up on the computer. There's got to be a glitch somewhere.

                                               Jessie

Saturday, March 15, 2008
Dear Diary,

    The home pregnancy test picks up this hormone, hCG, in the urine that's released only, ONLY, when you're pregnant. It's not in your body any other time. And even if the line is really faint on the test, it just means there's not a lot of the hormone in your system, and that you're not very far along. That doesn't matter though, considering mine stood out bold and proud. So, you can be pregnant and get a negative result if you're not very far along. You can have a false NEGATIVE; you can't have a false POSITIVE. And the blood tests are even more sensitive to the hormone than the home tests.

    Well, I'll see my doctor tomorrow, anyway. Although I'm

not sure what he's going to do. I guess he'll just refer me to someone else, because their hospital doesn't even have a maternity ward. Besides, he hasn't delivered a baby in years, the old geezer.

We had the sex lady from the health department come to our school my freshman year. She said that doctors who will care for underage pregnancies are hard to find, because malpractice insurance is so high, and we're considered high-risk cases. Western Baptist, last I heard, has a maternity ward, but no doctor that can treat me. And the only doctor Lourdes has won't accept a medical card. If I have to see her, how will we ever afford it?

Jessie

Sunday, March 16, 2008
Dear Diary,

We just got back from the doctor. He said the hCG, or whatever, in my bloodstream was really high, and there's no way I'm not pregnant. He recommended I see some Dr. Anunciato, the doctor from Lourdes. But when I was sent to another office to make the appointment, the secretary said she didn't take our insurance. Surprise. So she hung up with her and called Western Baptist. So now, I've got some Dr. Miller, or Muller, some name like that. I'll go there Wednesday. I'll bet it's some old man that won't do anything but be paid to ask how I'm doing every month. I've never had a good experience with a doctor. Ever. I don't like them. Maybe this guy will know what he's doing.

The nurse said that the ultrasound would give an educated guess at my due date. My life will end sometime around November 1st. It didn't look much like a baby at all. It looked more like an alien. Is it alright if I don't feel anything for this baby? I still don't believe it. Maybe that's it. When it finally sinks in and I know beyond a shadow of a doubt I'm pregnant, maybe I'll start to feel something.

Then again, if I can see a baby on an ultrasound and not believe I'm pregnant, it may not happen until I start to push.

But this isn't the best part of the day, by far. I told my Dad. And probably not in the best way, either. He was sitting in the waiting room while I was waiting for the pictures, and I came out and handed him one. I figured that would jumpstart the conversation, and he'd get it. He had to ask me what it was. That wasn't part of the plan.

"What do you think it is?"

"I don't know. What is it?"

"...Your first grandchild..."

His look killed me. Put a bullet through my heart. Of course it did Jess, you just put one through his. He mumbled, "You're pregnant." I nodded. "Who's the father? He has a responsibility!" He demanded I tell him. How could he ask me that? I'm not telling anyone who he is. It's my business. He didn't care about me; he just wanted to know where the father is.

I went out to the car, and just left him waiting there. It was ten minutes before he came out. Mamaw was sitting in the car and wanted to know where he was. I wasn't about to tell her yet. I just said that he was filling out papers, and he'd be a minute. When he came out, he looked like he was a hundred years old...

                                                    Jessie

<u>Tuesday, March 18, 2008</u>

Dear Diary,

I turned in my score today for Jones. As if I didn't feel horrible enough about everything that's going on, he insisted that we get our instruments out and perform my piece, since I was the only one done. I thought I would be clever and make a fugue out of the piece. I screwed that up to no end, and it sounded horrible. I just put my flute down and shook my head. That man was crazy to think we could do this. Or maybe I'm just a moron, and I'm the only one clueless.

One bad day to take my mind off an even worse situation. God must have a sense of humor.

Jessie

Wednesday, March 19, 2008
Dear Diary,

The doctor has an office attached to Western Baptist hospital. It's a small place. There was a little waiting room, and the short hallway leading to a few examining rooms. It had a nice atmosphere. There were paintings on the wall, a rock sculpture with a waterfall, and sofas and lounge chairs all over the place. The secretary was really nice. She took my insurance card and gave me papers to fill out. I didn't know how to fill out most of it. I left some answers blank. They never look at that stuff, anyway. I think it's more to keep you calm and out of their hair than for the information.

They finally took me back and took my blood pressure. They had to draw blood and get my weight before I was taken to the exam room. I had to take all my clothes off, as if I wasn't already nervous enough. I put on this little gown that, by the way, is NOT made for fat people, and had to be poked and prodded everywhere. I figured by the time the doctor got there, I wouldn't need to see him.

Dr. Madison wasn't at all the scary man I had feared, nor a man at all. She was really nice, and asked me if I was excited about the baby. She and the nurse looked kind of sad when I said,

Where My Ink Comes From

"I'm seventeen." Then she started telling me about how she had her twins when she was my age, and worse things could have happened. I don't know how much worse they can get, but if she insists...

But isn't that amazing? She's a DOCTOR now! And she had two of them! A nurse gave me a packet of information with a book that she had written, and it said that she did work for the military, too. If she can do all that with twins at my age, you think I could get a music major with just one?

I'm nervous. I didn't know when I took the steroids and the Benadryl and Pepto-Bismol that I was pregnant. I thought about telling her, but I didn't want her to think I was like the other girls I've talked about. I'm not. She said everything looked okay, anyway. So it doesn't really make a difference. It's bad enough that she saw my arms and wanted to know if she needed to prescribe me an antidepressant or recommend a shrink. I told her no. I hate going to any sort of doctor, and besides that, what legitimate shrink wouldn't send me off with one look at me?

I got to get another ultrasound. It was a lot better than the one I had at Crittenden. You could easily make out the head, and the little stubby arms and legs. It's still so tiny. I even saw it wiggle a little bit. It was almost cute. I got to keep some pictures of the ultrasound. I keep looking at it for any sign that I might fall in love at any given moment. At this rate, I don't think it's going to happen. I don't feel anything. It just doesn't seem real.

According to the ultrasound, I'm seven weeks pregnant today. I don't feel like it. I still feel normal. Physically, anyway.

I'm not ready for this.

Jessie

Where My Ink Comes From

Thursday, March 20, 2008
Dear Diary,
    Wow... I spoke way too soon. I woke up this morning and didn't even sit up in bed before I puked. And then I jumped up really quick, and my boobs are so sore, the motion made my whole chest ache. I can't stand it. Then I puked again, but managed to find the trash can that time. I took a shower last night, but I had to take another one this morning, change my bed sheets, and clean out the trash can. I'm in band now, and I'm still sick. I couldn't eat breakfast. I just took a vitamin with a glass of milk and went on.

    I went to see Holly this morning. I told her everything was official, and I was really pregnant. She wanted to know what my Dad said. I told her the truth – that he walks around the house, constantly looking like someone died. He told my grandmother, too. They're both hurting. I don't know what to tell them or how to make it any better. They didn't ask for this. She did offer some good advice, though. "You know how people are here at school. If you haven't told anyone, I wouldn't. It's a rule of thumb to wait until 12 weeks anyway, because so much can happen."

    What's going to happen? A miscarriage? I'm not that fortunate.

    ...Diary, what's wrong with me? How could I even say such a thing?! I don't want it to die. I want it to be born healthy, whether I feel like a mother or not. It deserves a chance just like everybody else, even if it did end up existing in the worst way possible.

                                             Jessie

Tuesday, March 25, 2008
Dear Diary,
    Time has stopped. I'm convinced the clock isn't moving

anymore. Things seem like they're moving so slowly now. And things keep getting worse and worse. I got into another fight with Taylor today. I can't take the stress anymore. People aren't helping me at all.

I called Blair after school. I decided I couldn't take it anymore, and broke down and told her I was pregnant. She didn't have much to offer me outside of prayer. I knew she couldn't do anything about it. I just wanted to tell someone.

I called Mom and told her. She didn't miss a beat between, "I'm pregnant," and, "DO YOU KNOW HOW HARD IT IS TO BE A SINGLE MOM?!" She thinks I'm so ignorant, like I don't know a baby is going to change my life. I don't know how yet, and no matter how hard people tell me it's going to be, I'm going to have to find out for myself, because there's no way I can imagine it.

I'm going to the doctor tomorrow. I wasn't supposed to go back for another week, but I'm getting scared. I'm afraid there's something wrong with the baby. I'm going to find out the results of the blood tests, and ask what other tests can be done. I've read about amniocentesis. It sounds painful, though. They actually put a needle through your stomach into your uterus to draw out the amniotic fluid to test for birth defects. If I wasn't so stupid to begin with, I wouldn't be so worried.

Jessie

Wednesday, March 26, 2008
Dear Diary,

I went to the doctor (again) today. Dr. Madison said all my tests results were normal. She said I could have the amniocentesis done if I really wanted to, but it has caused miscarriages before, and she didn't see the point. I guess I'll just take her advice and leave it at that.

I am officially eight weeks pregnant. I don't believe it. It really hasn't sunk in yet. I keep hoping and praying that this will all turn out to be a horrendous nightmare, or that I'll end up having a tumor that resembles a small baby. Only problem is, it keeps growing. Then again, tumors grow, right? I could have a malignant tumor, is all. I might not even be pregnant. That'd be nice, wouldn't it? My life is over either way, right?

I told Jones that everything is official. When this gets out, I'm going to be associated with the people that I absolutely hate. I've mentioned them before, you know the ones. I'm almost wondering why I haven't had an abortion yet. Isn't that awful? I don't know what I should do. I'd like to give it up for adoption, especially if Mary will take it. Am I a horrible person if I admit that I really don't want the baby? God, does that make me like my mother? I guess that's why I never wanted kids. It's in my blood to be a bad mother. If I tried to raise it myself, I might end up abusing it. And even if I don't really like kids, I hate to hear of a case on the news where some kid ends up dead or in the hospital. I don't want to be on there, too. No, I would never hurt it. Not intentionally. But what if it becomes too much, the kid pushes me to the breaking point? What then? I don't know what goes through a child abuser's mind; maybe that's how it starts.

I am absolutely sick at the thought. I was going to kill myself not too long ago. Now I'm supposed to make a decision for someone else? I hate to admit this, but I feel angry towards the baby. I know I shouldn't, and I'm mad at myself for feeling that way, but I can't help it, even if I don't have a reason to be angry. If I should be mad at anyone, it should be me. I screwed my own life up, and the baby didn't have a say.

Jessie

Wednesday, April 9, 2008
Dear Diary,

  Sorry for not writing.

  As of yesterday, I'm ten weeks. I can't keep anything down, and I have to hold onto my boobs just to sit up in the morning, they're so sore. Sorry for the graphics. I'm not sleeping, I'm living off popsicles, losing weight, I look like a zombie, and to add insult to injury, my dad still can't look me in the eye. My grandmother has gone into high gear though, making sure I'm eating and resting and watching every move I make. I think she's getting a little excited, now that the initial shock is over. I wish my dad would jump on that bandwagon with her.

  You know what really ticks me off? So far, not one person that knows I'm pregnant has asked me what I want. They've told me their horror stories, how bad I've messed up, but not ONE time has anyone ever just asked me what I thought was best, what I felt I needed to do. From the beginning, everyone has made the decision for me. I'm going to be a mother, or I'm going to be like my own mother. That's how that works. The only way out of this is death. I wouldn't have to kill myself. If I gave Mary the baby, having to deal with my dad and grandmother would kill me. They would absolutely hate me, and make it known that they did.

  I wish someone would have just asked. Or that I had a family that would understand that sometimes, the best thing a mother can do is let someone else be the mother. Would it not be enough to carry it for nine months, watch every little thing I did, and go through the pain (considering I fall in love by then) of giving it up? Oh, and after I go through this picnic called labor? I can't imagine that being any fun. I could get an abortion, but I'm not, because I don't want to kill what can't speak for itself. I don't have to do any of this, but that's not enough for them, is it? No, I'm going to have to raise a baby and it have a crappy life because

I'm going to have a crappy life. And I'll probably end up dropping out of school, becoming a child abuser, and going to prison where I'll be fried on Newschannel 6 until I get a death sentence by popular demand from the viewers.

You know what else ticks me off? I was on the pill. Well, the problem with the pill was that I wasn't taking it because I was planning on having sex. I took it for my periods, so I wasn't being rigid with the schedule of taking them at the same hour every day. Of course, now, I wish that I had.

Jessie

Thursday, April 10, 2008
Dear Diary,

I forgot to mention the GSA acceptance letters were postmarked on the 9th. I guess I'm a little anxious to see if I get in, even though I know it won't matter.

I played flute today for a little while. I'm going to miss these days...

Jessie

Friday, April 18, 2008
Dear Diary,

I don't know whether to cry or be absolutely overjoyed. My two year efforts have finally paid off. I got accepted into Governor's School for the Arts. And I can't even be happy about it.

I got a rejection letter, but it didn't say for what category, or if it was for both, or what. So I called them when I got home, and the woman said that the acceptance letters come in a package, and they usually take an extra day or two to get where they're going. She looked it up on her computer to see if I should expect one, and she said I got in. My packet should be in the mail tomorrow, I hope.

    I sent Mr. Jones a text message. I don't know if he got it or not, but I didn't hear back from him. I guess I'll see him Monday.

    I imagined being so much happier than this. When I got rejected last year, I vowed to get in. I said I was going to get into that school if it killed me. I'm the first to get accepted from our school, but it looks like I won't be the first to go.

Jessie

Saturday, April 19, 2008
Dear Diary,
    Still no packet. The mail won't come tomorrow either, since it'll be Sunday. Maybe Monday or Tuesday, not that it'll matter.

    Oh, and I'm still pregnant.

Jessie

Monday, April 21, 2008
Dear Diary,
    From my audition last year until now, I have worked hours and hours a day to get in. I thought last year that my mediocre 'talent' wouldn't get me anywhere, but I refused to have my pride shot in the head again with another rejection letter. If

after all this, I still didn't get better, I was going to quit. There was no point in wasting my time on something I would never achieve. So I give it all I have, practice five hours a day or more, giving up school and sleep, continuing on when my doctor kept telling me if I didn't stop playing, I would have to have surgery for my tendonitis, and for what? A piece of paper congratulating me on getting in, and they looked forward to having me as a student. That's great! Except by the time the school starts this summer, I'll be huge...

I knew I couldn't go when I found out I was pregnant. I'm stupid, I'm not ignorant. Apart from my Dad (and probably my doctor too, if I asked) never letting me go in a million years, you think GSA would want someone there like me?

Mr. Jones auditioned and didn't get in. He told me last year he would do cartwheels if I got in. I couldn't even get in his office this morning to tell him. He either didn't get the message, or he just doesn't care. I'm wagering the second. I wanted so badly to be his first student to get in. And when I told my Dad, he didn't say a word. He just nodded like his daughter hadn't achieved her two year dream. I told two people at school, one who didn't even smile before asking if I wanted to see her New York pictures, and the other only smiling and then going off with her boyfriend.

If Riley and Lauren were here from the academy, and Jordan and Brooke, this wouldn't have happened. We all would have gotten in together, and been proud to share one more summer. That's not going to happen now, because I screwed up. I haven't even talked to them. That summer we had together just seems like a dream now, like it never even happened. I didn't want to leave when I was there, because I knew what I would have to come home to. Driving away, I remember looking in the rearview mirror at the lights of the school until they blurred with the lights of the city, and I watched them fade away until I couldn't see them at all anymore. I miss them so much, it hurts.

There's nothing for me here. When I was at that

academy, I knew what happiness was, for the first time. Nobody knew me up there; nobody knew my past, or my thoughts. I could be a whole different person. I've never had everybody be my friend before. And it's not that I was popular, that wasn't it. That's just how it was, for everyone. We were all happy for the success the other had. We were all friends with each other, and no one was left out. And I'd give anything to go back to that.

So nobody cares that I got into this school. Nobody cares that I worked so hard for so long, nobody cares that I wanted to make them all proud, that I gave it everything I had, or even that I'm hurting. I hate being alone. I've learned that you can only rely on yourself, that you shouldn't depend on other people. That's when I'm the weakest. But it kills me inside to be alone.

Jessie

Tuesday, April 22, 2008
Dear Diary,

Last night didn't go too smoothly. My brother was running through the house screaming again, and he got Mamaw upset. He broke the picture she had of her husband from when he was in the air force by throwing the TV remote at it. I couldn't believe it! It was all my grandmother had left of him. It went straight through the photo, and I wanted to knock him stupid when he just casually went, "Oh, I didn't think it would break." How ignorant do you have to be? By the way, I'm not talking about a little brother who might not know better, for whatever reason. This is a 19 year old, high school drop-out, lazy bum who wouldn't know he had a job if he carried it around in his pocket. All he does all day is play videogames and terrorize everyone in the house.

I know a lot of Mamaw's bad health is because of all the

strokes she's had, but there's no doubt in my mind that he's to blame for her getting worse. Of course, I don't have any right to accuse anyone else. I did cause my dad's heart attack, right? I can't imagine being any better than my brother.

    I hadn't told my dad I loved him in years. The doctor didn't think he would live through his open-heart surgery, and I remember while we waited for it to be over, I sat in the waiting room and tried to count how many opportunities I had to say it, and never did. Well, I did after that day. That was August of last year, 2007, and I never let a chance slip. With the way Eric is, it was difficult for my dad to recover. He comes home from the hospital, and my brother is there waiting to call him a lazy, worthless bum who'll never amount to anything.

    Worthless bum... Let me tell you something about my dad: When Mom left, he raised us on a 3rd grade education, he worked himself into heart problems and still managed to keep us fed and in school, he went on welfare, he got food stamps, he had to admit he needed help to raise us, and at the same time, his mother's getting worse, and he had to move in with her, all of us, to take care of her. By the way, while he's doing this, he built us a two-story house BY HIMSELF (as in, he tore an old house down for lumber and built a house, not hiring anybody to help him), and was nearly killed during that construction. He never stopped going to Nashville to make it as a musician so we would have a better life. While my brother lays up in bed all day without a job and nothing better to do than make life miserable for us, my dad is trying to make ends meet when he STILL hasn't gotten over his surgery. I try to help him all I can, because Eric says he doesn't feel like he owes my Dad anything else for raising him. I have to get outside and help him mow the yard, and carry heavy things back and forth from the two houses. And if you think that's changed since I'm pregnant, think again. He still needs my help. Tell me, who sounds like the lazy bum in this picture?

    I tried so long not to hate my brother. I knew if I ever

started hating him, I'd never stop, and I'd certainly never forgive him. Although, I really don't care about forgiving him for him. I could care less what happened to him. I hope that someday, I can forgive him... because I have to move on. Come next fall, I'm out of here, college bound. But I have to leave everyone else behind to fend for themselves. My dad has always wanted to go to Arizona, so I keep telling him to hang on until I can get out of college, and I'll buy him a house wherever he wants to go. And if Arizona's it, then that's where I'll send him. My aunt Donna wants Mamaw to come live with her someday. As for my brother... let sleeping dogs lie...

    I haven't prayed in a long time. I know I don't deserve anything God has to offer me. But last night, I managed to just ask that He not make me raise my baby in this house, not even until I leave for college. I look at me, and how I've turned out. I know I can't blame Eric for anything I've done, but I'm ready to blame him for every single ounce of pain I've ever felt from being in that house. He never made me cut myself, he never made me take those pills, but he always made me feel the way I felt. I don't know how I'll ever be able to forgive him. I don't think I ever will.

    You know... I really, really miss the academy. Whether or not they really cared, it was easy to make myself believe they did. And now, I have to go through it all again; losing someone and having to face the reality that I'm all alone, and I always have been and will be. When I think about them, I get that feeling. Anyone who's really been hurt knows it. It's when your chest just goes numb and hot, and you're convinced your heart is literately breaking in two.

    I wish the most I had to worry about was getting to school on time and remembering to feed the dogs. I called Jordan last night and he talked about how much he missed elementary school, when there was no responsibility... and my brother was somewhat sane... But why did we want that to end so badly? Maybe if we had known, we wouldn't have been able to accept the end. But that's a stupid thought, right? That's in the past.

I made a vow a long time ago that I wouldn't rely on anyone else. Maybe that's another reason I love keeping a diary so much, since it will still be around tomorrow (my pen will quit if I keep talking). My razor never left me, either. When I couldn't listen to the yelling anymore, one quick slice, and I was okay for the moment. Friends are great, but one day, you'll wake up, and everything you thought you knew will be all wrong. Every time I have to recover form something like that, it takes a little more of me away. I can't keep doing that. I have to do everything in my power to deliver a healthy baby, and that means staying away from everything that's going to add any more stress to an already bad situation.

Jessie

Wednesday, April 23, 2008
Dear Diary,

I'm in Band now, and my director is upset. I don't blame him. And I can't really say anything, since I'm one of the people he's upset about for not showing up for band practice. Maybe I can stop puking long enough to go Thursday for an hour and a half. At least I can say that I really want to go. It's not that I'm missing just to be missing. I would love to spend a little extra time away from home. Maybe I'm not sick from being pregnant as much as I am sick of worrying all the time. I'm sick of a lot of things these days...

I've been practicing at home, anyway. The last three days, I haven't been able to find my Flute (oh, I'm sure it's at home somewhere in the junk), which is really unlike me, because I practice everyday I can. I'm not too far behind on my music. There's a spot on *Japanese Fantasy* that's getting in my way, but

Where My Ink Comes From

I'll nail it in a little while. Now that I don't have any auditions coming up for once, and nobody to really answer to, I can spend more time on my music.

   You know what really gets me? I've never admitted this out loud before, but I'm really starting to hate Band. Don't misunderstand, though. I love playing with everything I am, and I love music. It's all that's saved me in the past. But when I came to the high school in 8th grade to play in the Pep Band, it was a blast. Everybody got along, we all had our inside jokes, and we were all friends with everybody else. At least, I thought so. My freshman year, it all went downhill. The seniors we had when I was in middle school left, and after the seniors of my freshman year graduated, we really lost something. It could just be me – and the way I am lately, it probably is – but it just seems like the Band just isn't any fun anymore.

   Now, we have cliques in the Band. If someone had told me that in 8th grade, I would have been rolling on the ground laughing. Everyone has their own little group, and it's no fun that way. Not a lot of people left really have a lot of respect for anyone else. I'll be fair; not everybody's gotten that way, but most have. And we have freshman that can be unbelievably annoying. Again, I'll be fair and say they aren't stupid. One even wrote the composition that we'll be performing in our concert. You know... ...maybe it is me. The director just put emphasis on "Your Band is only as good as your weakest player." That would be me, right?

   You want to hear another secret? I can't use the A flat key on my flute. That's it. If I need to play A flat, I go silent. And I can't count rhythm. (That one hurt to say.) Sure, I CAN eventually...after getting out about 30 caGCulators and writing in each and every note value. Oh, and screw high and low notes. Ledger lines are the devil. I hate them with a passion, because I can't read them. And yet, get this, I have perfect pitch. Not afraid to admit that, I'm kind of proud. I have perfect pitch; I can take a

Where My Ink Comes From

piece and dominate it. I have beautiful vibrato, and I think that's what landed me the acceptance letter. But not until I've sat down for what feels like 20 years and gone over and over and over and over it again and again. And I get so angry at the seniors who just sit down with some major composition and ace it the first try. And I'm willing to bet that I practice more! But that's only because I'm not as good as they are in the first place, right? That just means I'll have to try harder than the rest.

  I've always thought that I was the weak link in the Band's chain. I feel like I am. So I'll just sit in the front of the class, play the lowest octave note I can, and pray I'm never heard to be corrected. If I have to play by myself, or even in a small group with other instruments and I think I'm going to be heard, I freeze. I know the part. I'm just too embarrassed to play. But then I get so mad! Because as low as I think of myself, I go home and rock out! I can beatbox! I can play stuff that I never dreamed in a million years I'd be good enough to play! And for what? I play the first four notes of the D scale on the lowest octave so that I look like I'm playing something if I get lost so Mr. Jones won't call on me.

  Newsflash, by the way; I'm NOT the Band's favorite person. I fight constantly with Taylor, I depend too much on Blair for all the answers to my problems, and the freshman drummers are enough to drive anyone to suicide on some days, they're so obnoxious. And it doesn't help that I'm the only Flute, either. I'm not in any clique; I'm thought of as too weird, stupid, bothersome, fill in the blank. I'm different. I'm not sure how, but I know I am. I can't fit in with anyone. When the preps don't want you, that's one thing... But when the nerds and the geeks knock you out... that's sad... And you know by now, I can't keep a friend. That's why I'm so much better off alone.

  I'm not doing Band next year. I haven't told anyone yet. I've said I'm going to quit so often before, they have no reason to believe me now. But I've made up my mind, and I'm absolutely sure this is what I want to do. I'll miss it, but I miss what it should be, and what it was those years ago. Don't get me wrong, though; I'll never quit my music. I've got too much riding on it to quit. But coming in here everyday to the same thing is just getting old. Besides, I'll still be in concert band, and I'll get to play once in a while. But I've got a baby on the way, so what's the point in even trying for marching and pep band? But I will NEVER stop playing. Ever. Like I've said, if I can't do my music in heaven, then I don't want to go there.

      What good am I in practice? I never play while I'm in there. Only at home, in my tiny little room when no one's home, and the only time I'm ever good enough for anybody to listen is when there isn't anybody there. Some musician...

                                                    Jessie

Saturday, April 26, 2008
Dear Diary,

      On the plus side of my brother having an up-all-night schedule, he's asleep during the day. That always makes for a peaceful day. He's supposed to go stay with my Aunt Donna Monday and come back hopefully never. This week should be smoother.

      I'm starting to pick out names. I still don't believe I'm pregnant. I'm just playing along until this nightmare is over. "Dream on," that's what I keep telling myself. I know I'm never going to wake up. I just keep hoping...

      I've got Iris, Rachael, and Zoey picked out if it's a girl. For a boy, Caden or Bentley. I guess a girl will get my middle name, and a boy will get my dad's. Or I like Benjamin for a boy. Those are all subject to change. But I think I'm going to wait a long time still before I look at names again. I'm still not happy or accepting yet, and picking out a name is something that's supposed to be exciting and selective. When I'm not happy, I'm not caring what I name the kid. And everyone deserves a name that means something, right? I hate my name, because it doesn't mean anything important. I want my baby's name to have meaning, something reflective.

    Does this mean I'm starting to care?

                                                    Jessie

Monday, April 28, 2008
Dear Diary,

    "It's noble, but it's stupid." That's the newest quote from Dawson McAllister, a radio show I listen to. I liked it, because it can apply to so many things; like not telling anyone who the father of my baby is because I'm afraid of how my sick family will react. It's noble, but it's stupid, isn't it? My daughter or son needs to know the truth eventually, and I guess I shouldn't have to carry this burden alone. Well, I've always done things by myself. This shouldn't be any different.

    Is it stupid to try to protect everyone from the truth? It may be noble to take pain for someone else, but is it stupid? I stayed up with my dad the whole night I told him, scared to death he was going to have another heart attack. Noble. Who's the father? He moved, he's oblivious, he doesn't know. Stupid? What if lying about who the father is now leads to more complications later when the truth DOES come out? My dad might eventually find out, and I don't think his heart can handle it. And in the meantime, how can I do this by myself...?

                                                    Jessie

Where My Ink Comes From

Tuesday, April 29, 2008
Dear Diary,

    It's like Dawson asked at the last show. Which came first, the chicken or the egg? Was I depressed first, or did someone leave me that started this vicious cycle? I don't remember much about my childhood. I think I've managed to suppress most of it. I guess when I was 12 and things just got so bad, I forgot about the good memories, if there even was any. I think I want to know what happened. All I've heard are the stories Mamaw told me, and with her mind the way it is, I have no reason to believe any of it is even a fraction of the truth. Dad has never said anything to back her up, and Mom says she's not telling the truth. I want to remember it, not to just hear from someone who thinks they know.

    The stories were awful. Mom came home drunk and threw me against the wall when I was a few months old, she let all her weekend boyfriends screw around with me (by the way, she's telling this to a 4 year old), she locked me in closets for hours… you don't tell stuff like that to a little kid. I started to hate Mom for a long time, until I started questioning Mamaw's reliability. I spent a summer with her when I got a birthday card out of the blue three years ago, and now, I just don't know. It's hard to believe that after all these years, she can waltz right back in and be a mom again. Then again, did she really have a choice? Dad and Mamaw took her through hell and high water to keep us away from her, and her dad paid for our lawyer. She didn't have an attorney, short of the free one the state provided, which she swears threw the case for her.

    Sometimes, I'm not sure I even want to remember. They always say that what we don't know won't hurt us. And I don't think I could take the weight of knowing the truth. It might destroy what I think I already know.

                                                Jessie

Where My Ink Comes From

Wednesday, April 30, 2008
Dear Diary,

It doesn't come off so easily that I'm miserable. At least, I don't think so. Nobody knows what I think, feel, the things I do, no one knows. Nobody's worried, and I'm alright by myself. I miss the things I've had in the past, but the keyword there is PAST. This is NOW. What can I do now to make sure I never have to be hurt like that again? Be lonely? Never have to worry about anyone but myself? Give up one everyone else? Being a loner hurts. Never believe anyone that says it doesn't bother them. It really, really hurts. But that's my point! Do I really need anyone? I think I do sometimes, but I'm not so sure. When I get out of my desperate state, I remember that I can be independent, as I have been most of my life. I just have to learn to rely on myself. I'm going to be a mother, and I can't have distractions like that get in my way.

                                                 Jessie

Friday, May 2, 2008
Dear Diary,

I haven't heard this song yet, but I'm listening to it now. It's called *Who am I?* by Casting Crowns. Sometimes, I wonder if they're just really good, or if God is really speaking through them.

I just... I've been wondering lately if maybe it's not too late to go back. You know, like to church and everything. I've always said that I'd done too much for Him to ever take me back, that I'm just too much of a repeat offender, so to speak. When I have tried to follow Him, it was just so hard. And is our best really good enough? Does a true Christian screw up day to day, think and do the things I do? When I tried, I would end up cutting, or suicidal; not because of, but in spite of. And I'd think, this isn't something you do when you're saved. How can a Christian sin repeatedly and do what God wants at the same time? Then I'd think, am I really that tough? He could fix my problems easier than I can blink. But what about me? He fixes everything, then what do I do? That's it? "Thanks God, but I have to go. Going to slit my wrist today." I almost wonder if I tried hard enough.

    I wrote a song a while back, *God Sends Angels*, about God sending people to do His work when He's too busy. Blair was the first angel. It's so obvious that she loves God, and I'll admit for the first time, I'm jealous of her. I know I shouldn't be. I know I could have it too, if I tried hard enough. When I think I can try and do it, there's still that voice in my head going, stop cutting. Stop planning your death, and then maybe you and God can talk. Blair tried to tell me it was Satan. I don't know if I believe that or not. It's the truth, right? Then again, that's what he does. But Blair, she loves everybody. I've never heard her say one cross thing about anybody. She's the epitome of a Christian. She never swears, never raises her voice. I've told her not to get angry, because quiet anger is worse than R rated anger. But if she can do it, why can't I?

    I wonder of God ever reads my journal... It might help me explain things...

Jessie

Friday, May 2, 2008
Dear Diary,
  This is the song I was talking about earlier:

God Sends Angels

I won't forget the day,
She sat next to me,
Heaven only knows what she was thinking.
I don't remember how we got off,
But she started talking about God,
My shifty eyes must have gave it away.
She said if I didn't remember anything else,
To know that He was waiting for me,
With his arms wide open,
And that was all I needed to hear.

Chorus
God found me, He sent her,
To a classroom bench to bring me to Him,
He found me when I thought I was alone.
He knew when He saw me,
Sitting alone,
Exactly what she needed to say.
I think God sends angels.

It's been a few years now,
Since that day's been here.
Between then and now,
So much has happened.
Everyday, the memories I face,
I wish I could forget all my mistakes.
I remember the night I wanted to.
It took a really kind heart to pull me back.

When he made that call, he saved my life.
I wish I could tell him,
All he really did for me that night.

<u>Chorus</u>
God found me, He sent him,
To a telephone,
And I made a call,
He didn't know he was saving a life.
I knew when he said it,
I would be okay,
I knew I never once had walked alone.
I think God sends angels.

<u>Bridge</u>
Don't think that you can't,
Help someone who needs someone.
And don't give up the fight,
You've fought for so long.
Don't lose the hope or faith,
You hold in your hand.
God is in control.

<u>Chorus</u>
God finds us, He sends us,
Angels when He knows,
We need them,
He sends us help when we can't help ourselves.
I knew when He sent me,
Those angels, He saved me,
God finds ways to save our lives everyday.
I think God sends angels.

I know he sends angels,

Where My Ink Comes From

Angels.

I won't forget the day,
She sat next to me.
Heaven only knows what I was thinking,
When I looked at her,
And said, "Keep believing."

      I wasn't sure how to say 'sat on a heater,' so I just called it a classroom bench. I'm not sure too many people would know what that is. Even I don't know what it is.
      Blair, like I said, was the first angel. I wasn't going through anything in particular at that time, but I was just fighting my demons off, as I typically am doing. The second angel was difficult to explain. I actually called him that night. It was Jones, and I wasn't too sure what I was thinking when I called him, but I did. And I was going to kill myself that night, and the only reason I didn't was because he had to go and he said, "We're going to talk about this tomorrow." And I didn't want to die before I tried one more time to hear something that would talk me out of it. Of course, I didn't tell him this. I still haven't. It's my secret.
      ...I've noticed that I have a lot of secrets, actually...

                                                                  Jessie

<u>Monday, May 5, 2008</u>
Dear Diary,
      I took the AP exam this morning for Government and Politics. I wonder if they give sympathy grades? It hurts just thinking about it. I probably left 10 or 15 blank, and 2 of the open responses, I didn't even attempt. I had absolutely no clue. I know you always give your best effort, but I literally had never heard

those terms they wanted me to describe, there was no reference, and if I didn't know what they were, I certainly couldn't explain how they worked. I finally stopped on the third. I figured by then, they already knew I was an idiot. What's really bad is, I DID study. I always do. Each test, each quiz, I study for. I just naturally suck at tests.

    I had a playing test in band, too. That one was fun. I'm a little lucky, I guess. Jones gave me only a few measures to play, indicating by then, he was tired of administering stupid playing tests. And given it wasn't perfect, I got a 98. Then he said something about working stylistically with me. What does that mean? I probably do need to work on that, but how about the fact that I can't count? How about, I can't read ledger notes? Of course, there is that little part where those are my secrets.

    As much as I would like to fix that stuff, I've waited so long to do it; I'd be embarrassed to ask. I just know I'd hear, "You waited this long to tell me that? Get with it!" Don't think I haven't tried to fix it on my own. Believe me, I have. But there comes a time in every Bando's life where they know that no amount of practice, no book that can be read, no repair that can be made, no new instrument part can be bought that's going to fix your problem. And then you go to your band director, who has this tendency to make you feel an inch high when you've missed just about every rehearsal and then come asking him for help. Yeah, I think I'll just try to remedy it a little bit, like I always have. I usually just play an octave down, or just pretend to be playing. So while everyone else is playing *English Folk Fantasy*, I'm playing *Come to Jesus* in whole notes in the lowest register I can get it in. And I ask myself why I still suck after hours and hours and hours of practice...

    I can't wait until this year's over. Three more weeks. Just three. And I'll never have to go back to that room again. I loved that room in middle school. I have so many good memories there. And maybe I'm just being overly dramatic, but it seems like the one thing that kept me sane all these years is driving me to insanity. Am I playing this right? Can they hear me? I don't want them to hear me! Is he looking? He's going to say something. He never has, why would he now? Don't make him say it three times! It's ridiculous! I have never in my life dreaded opening my flute case like I have this past year.

    I've already made up my mind. I'm going to go in there everyday from now on and play as well as I can, just like I do at home, and I'm not going to give a crap in the world about who can hear what. I don't care if I'm so wrong, I don't sound like I'm playing the right song. I'm going to go in there, and I'm going to play, and come the end of the year, win, lose, or draw, I never have to go back again, so it won't matter what anyone comes to think of me. Caring stopped when two pink lines showed up. I'm just tired. I don't want to care anymore.

    Is it natural for me to be this afraid? I know every new mom must have a fear, but my case is so unique. How afraid can I be and still be normal? I'd give anything if I could tell someone the truth. I mean, Jones, Holly, and Blair all know I'm pregnant, but nobody knows about the father, or how or when it happened. I'm not sure if I want someone to know. That was the first thing Jones asked me. "Who's the father?" I just told him I couldn't tell him that. And I can't. I want to, but my well-being is hanging by a thread as it is without everything else falling apart.

                                                    Jessie

Tuesday, May 6, 2008
Dear Diary,
    Mary gave some stuff to my Dad to give to me. I got a few baby outfits and some much-needed pants. She swears she's going to be in the delivery room. She really wants to be. I don't

know. I think whenever I get something like that, or I go to the doctor, hear the heartbeat, see the ultrasound, watch or feel it move, it all sinks a little deeper in. I still can't believe it. Yeah, you'd think by now, I would have accepted it and moved on. But I just can't believe I'm pregnant. I can't. I just want to pretend I'm a kid for a little while longer.

    I'm starting to show. Bad. I don't have to wear maternity clothes yet, but I choose to because they usually don't look like maternity, and they hide that ever-elusive baby bump well. A girl asked me the other day (a stupid freshman, no doubt) if I was pregnant. I got upset later, but at the time, I acted like she'd struck a nerve and said, "So what? Fat people are automatically pregnant? I get Rosie O' Donnell is going have triplets! Stupid freshman..." Everyone laughed. It was funny for a minute. Then I realized, people really CAN tell I'm pregnant. I can't imagine what I'll look like when I go to Owensboro. I'll be as big as a house in June, and July... I gave up GSA. I won't give up Owensboro. It's only for a week. I can handle a week, right? And nobody ever died from missing a recital. The opposite usually occurs at mine. The survivors are the ones that don't go. I could make Beethoven cry on piano...

    Mary and my grandmother wanted to come with me when I went to the doctor. They want to see the ultrasound. Maybe I'll find out what I'm having.

    You know... When each day is over, I'm still unhappy. I haven't accomplished anything. I haven't made the day mean a thing. People assumed I wanted to keep the baby, and I was never asked what I wanted to do, or what I felt was best. Mary wanted to take the baby. Open, closed adoption won't matter. And it would know I was her real mother, and I loved him enough to give him up for a better life for him (or her). Dad and Mamaw aren't going to be the ones raising her. It'll be me. And if I have to drop out of school to take care of her, neither one of us are in for a good life. How do I tell them without Dad killing over from heart problems, or Mamaw stroking out? Do I just go with it? Become a mother? Screw what I want. I chose to have sex, I chose to get knocked up, right? I made the mistake. I deserve my punishment.

And you know what else? I wish it had been that way. If this had to happen, I wish the father was a normal father, I was having a normal pregnancy, my friends all ditched me because their mothers told them that I was a bad influence, I had the baby and stayed in school because my parents couldn't stand to see me go this far to give up, and why not? We get married, live in a run-down trailer in some campground, and have waffles on our anniversary. Perfect! But oh no, the father is some walking mass of ignorance who's got everyone eating out of the palm of his hand. You know what he called HIS BABY? A bastard child. He called his baby, my baby, a bastard child. If that's what my child is destined to be, she'll have gotten it from him.

I had to cut over it. I couldn't stop myself. What right...
...He didn't care about my rights. He has no rights. He doesn't have the right to breathe the same air as I do. I can't forgive what he's done. I never can. I won't. And when MY baby's born, and I'm holding her, he's going to come and want to hold it, and everyone's just going to expect me to hand her over like, "Sure! Hold your bastard child!" All I can say is, I'd better be having a girl, because I don't want to bring another asshole into this world...

Jessie

Wednesday, May 7, 2008
Dear Diary,
We went on a field trip today to the courthouse to watch sentencing of felony cases. It was okay, until the judged ticked

everyone off by letting a sex offender go with 30 DAYS IN JAIL! No, I'm sorry. I meant 5 years, in which he can get out after 30 days for something called shock probation. You know what that is? The judge explained that it's when a little time spent in jail is supposed to scare you into straightening your life up, so you don't have to serve full time. What kind of garbage is that? That little girl he raped is in a group home now, because she's tried to kill herself three times and that guy can't figure out why her family is having problems with her. Where's the justice for that little girl? She'll never forget what happened to her, so why does she get a life sentence, while he gets a slap on the hand? You know what's going to happen when he gets out? "No, your Honor," *laugh* "I'll never do THAT again!" Is that judge stupid? Wow... God bless America...

You know, Riley went to several countries last summer. And he has the best answer yet for stopping crime. Are you ready for this? An eye for an eye. Yeah. If you steal something, they'll cut your hand off. If you burn someone's house down, your house is given to the family you made homeless. Kill someone, they kill you back. If you rape someone, say goodbye to your manhood. THAT'S justice.

I got into an argument with Taylor today that was so stupid, I had to ask her what she said, because I knew it couldn't have been what I heard. She said that wouldn't work, because Americans are really competitive, and crime rate would soar as more people tried to do things and get away with them. Now, I believe that everyone has the right to have an opinion, but get real. As least have a sensible point of view. I mean, how stupid! Yeah, let me go rape this kid so that when I get away, I can brag about it to all my friends.

You know how there's a sex offender registry? I think there should be a stupid people registry. For people who give dumb opinions like this girl had, the people who let the stupid people off, and those responsible for those labels on the silicone that say, "DO NOT EAT." And President Bush would be the first in line to sign up, followed by the guy who stole a Snickers Bar so he could go brag about it. "What happened to your hand, man?" "Oh, I stole a candy bar. Pretty cool, huh?"

And by the way, there'd be a justice system for stupid people. Those that truly want to change would have shock collars. You know, like a dog. And we'd watch and wait for that look in their eye that says they're about to do something that just doesn't make sense. And zzzzzzzttt!! "Sorry, you had that look."

Oh, I like days like this when I can find at least one little thing to laugh at. I need to start laughing more...

Jessie

Thursday, May 8, 2008
Dear Diary,

The only day worse than Monday is Thursday. Because it feels like Friday all day long, until you come to that harsh reality that you have one more day left.

If stress causes miscarriages, I'm a working miracle. I forgot to mention that one. I had to go to the hospital Tuesday. I started spotting. My doctor said to come in for an ultrasound when I called her, but when the nurse looked at me, she said everything looked so good, they didn't even need to do one. I had stopped bleeding before I'd ever known I was in the first place, so it wasn't a big deal. I have to go back to see my doctor Monday.

I've been writing a lot lately. Not just in my journal, but my notebooks and everything. I don't know... It's like my head is so full, I can get part of the information down, and then move on to the next bit. I'd have more than a novel if I ever wrote everything. But at the same time, I don't think I can ever fix any of it. I know I can't. I was writing last night about my amazing ability to get myself out of absolutely anything. Even when I had finished scraping the bottom of the barrel, I would always find something worth hanging on to. This is probably the only mistake, the worst mistake that I can't get myself out of. Of course, I would always say that, too. But am I really right this time? I had two bottles of aspirin and a letter to absolutely no one. I didn't feel the need to say goodbye to anyone, if no one cared at all. I would have done it. I had the time and day. There wasn't any backing out. And there it was, a test I had believed with every ounce of my being would be negative. That aspirin is still where I left it; in the very back of my bottom dresser drawer. How long will it sit there?

    I don't want to be a mother. I want to go to college, make a future for myself in music, and live life the way I want to live it, without any pain or any fear like I've always had to live with. I've got a life sentence now. From now on, there's always going to be pain. I'm always going to have my doubts and my phobias, and I'll probably always have to depend on a blade. That wasn't the life I wanted. I promised myself that if I could get through school, I could buy a house as far away from here as possible, get that huge bathroom I've always wanted, get a dog and a cat, play my music, not give a care about anyone but myself for a little while, and finally live the good life that I've always wanted, or at least a decent one would be nice. No, I've got responsibility now, don't I? Screw the house, screw my music, and screw getting out of here. I'm stuck here for the rest of my life.

    You see that? You see how selfish I am? Listen to me. I don't care about the baby, I only care about myself. Reason number 624,673,252 for hating myself with a passion.

Jessie

Thursday, May 8, 2008
Dear Diary,
  I have Good Charlotte's *Hold On* blaring in the headphones...
    ...No one has noticed...
Jessie

Friday, May 9, 2008
Dear Diary,
  I have to read my paper out loud to the class today, and why, I don't know. It does me absolutely no good. Anytime Jones has us do peer review, someone just catches a typo or something, and they don't tell me what's wrong with it or what I need to change. The only thing that happens is it scares the absolute crap out of me.
  I really, really need to get over the whole 'shy' thing. I mean, everyone has a degree of it I guess, but I'm ridiculous. I won't even look friends in the eye, at least when I had them. I'm bent on getting out of here without anyone remembering who I am. High school reunion? What's that? I'm not even going into the yearbook. I take a horrible picture, and every year, it's just one more photo I'm dumb enough to sit and be hung up on because I look pathetic.
  I had a dream last night about Stephanie. She was my first friend. Ever. I couldn't forget her if I wanted to. She was also the first loss. We were best friends until 5th grade. We started drifting in 3rd, but I held on until the very end. I tried so hard. In the end, all I did was make all her new friends mad and I had to give up. We would talk about when we were little, how we would die for each other if we had to, but then we wouldn't want to go on without the other. We had both had pretty rough starts in life,

so we were pretty deep for little kids. It probably still didn't mean anything, but other people didn't get us for it, so we just stuck close by each other. When I lost her, I didn't have anyone else to cling to. I didn't even have a mom at that time, and I viewed my dad as a social problem like any other 10 year old. I had absolutely nobody. I wasn't ready to walk alone. And after that, it just seemed like everyone I met ended up disappointing me. Maybe I was afraid of losing them like I had lost the only person I ever really loved, and I was just too clingy for anyone to handle for very long.

    Come to think of it, my problems in childhood started with her. Letters started pouring in in fourth grade from my teacher on how strange I was acting. Of course I was weird. I had lost the only person I cared about. It doesn't matter if you're four or forty, losing someone you love hurts more than any feeling imaginable. Stephanie still hurts. She eventually moved to Michigan, and believe it or not, I still call her time to time. But I know that she's got her friends up there, and probably doesn't even remember my name until I call. And she's never tried to call me. Maybe it's that desperate kid that I used to be still trying to get through to her. I still don't want to let her go, and it's been so long.

    I said we both had rough starts in life. We had similar stories as far as our mothers go. In fact, according to her, her father had told her mom that they were leaving at three o' clock that day for Michigan, and if she wanted to continue being a mother and being part of that family, then she needed to be there. She never showed up. Later, her mom was working at Wal*Mart, and I ran into her. She told my grandmother that he never told her that they were leaving, and she fought so hard to stay with her kids. After that, I found myself wondering if the same happened with my own mom.

    Regardless of how similar our lives were to begin, we both turned out very different. Stephanie ended up with a drug problem, and I ended up with a baby. We both like blades more than we should though. Well, maybe apart from the whole 'baby' thing, we aren't that different. She chose acid, I chose Zoloft.

Jessie

<u>Saturday, May 10, 2008</u>
Dear Diary,

    I did something really weird today. And if it's weird for me, you know it's out there. But today, I actually felt a little smidge of excitement, just a smidge and just for a split second, about the baby. But as soon as I felt it, it was immediately followed by, "Can't take care of myself, how do I take care of someone else?" "I'm too psychotic to handle a baby." "How do I afford diapers?" "I've heard formula costs a fortune, too." "A job, motherhood, AND school?" "Single mom, single mom." That's my problem. I'm too caught up in how I'm going to make this work to be happy about a little bundle. Maybe I
got excited at the thought of this being over more than I am the thought of having a baby. And I felt the first little flutter today, so that's probably what set me off.

    But you know, even feeling the flutter, seeing the ultrasound, I still don't feel anything. I don't. I still don't believe I'm even pregnant. Am I crazy?

    Well, first trimester is over. Let me tell you how fast that flew by. I'm still living off popsicles and graham crackers; I can't keep anything else down. I don't keep all of that down. Dr. Madison gave me something for the morning sickness, but a lot of good that's done. I get to go back Monday for a checkup, anyway. That'll give me something to look forward to.

Jessie

Monday, May 12, 2008
Dear Diary,

  The doctor's appointment went well. Not that we do anything special, really. I get weighed, poked, prodded, and asked if I have any questions. I say no, thinking about the million questions I have, and she lets me go on my merry way.

  No, doc, nothing you can answer for me. But here are my questions. Why? Why, out of the hundred girls at school who have unprotected sex a dozen times, with no life goals and no plans short of going to school until they can legally drop out, me, one time and on the pill, why do I end up being the one, out of all of them, who gets pregnant? And why is it that God chose me to be someone's mother when I can't even take care of myself, let alone a baby, and when I'm so screwed up, I was going to kill myself a couple of months ago?

  Why choose me? There are families right now that have been trying to get pregnant for years and years and can't, and women that can get pregnant who can take care of a baby a lot better than I can. Don't you understand this baby's life is going to be horrible, because I can't make a life for her that would be worth anything? So why did God choose me? Why me?

                Jessie

Friday, May 16, 2008
Dear Diary,

  I knew we were overdue for the end-of-the-year drama. So, we have a bunch of students protesting against our vice principal not being principal, since ours is quitting this year, and over Mrs. Holly not getting to teach senior English. A bunch of students walked out of the classrooms Tuesday and Wednesday so they could stand out on the front lawn and look stupid. They succeeded in the 'looking stupid' department. And they've got her upset over it. She was scared to death she was going to lose her job. And Jones finally told her, "You got a pink slip yet? You got a schedule for next year? You got a job." She hasn't been here that long. Her first year was my freshman year, and the ones that haven't been there too long are the ones that are more likely to lose their job if something goes wrong, so I don't blame her for worrying. But really, there's nothing to worry about. She didn't do anything wrong. Shut up Holly, you're fine...

    Speaking of Jones, I got yelled at today. And I've never been happier. He actually yelled at me WHILE WE WERE PLAYING to tell me I sounded good. That has NEVER happened before. Of course, then when he said my name, I panicked, and put a stake through the heart of my music, but up until that point, I got him to yell at me because I did something right for once.

    By the way, I haven't been writing because I've been too busy to breathe. I missed school yesterday and Monday. I went to apply for financial aid yesterday at Community Based Services, or whatever. They have this TANF thing, Temporary Assistance for Needy Families, and Mary told me I could get it. I can't get it until the baby's born, and then I have to name the father and work so many hours a week. Now, let's look at why I wanted that in the first place... 1) So I could be a mom and stay in school. 2) So I wouldn't have to pay a babysitter for 12 hours straight. And 3) Because I can't get a job and pay for anything! Not to mention, the father is the LAST PERSON I want in the picture. The last. The last. The last. That will be hell on earth.

    I was counting on this. My whole plans were right on this. Now what am I supposed to do? I could go through with all that, but that's the equivalence of dropping out of school to work. And that's what I'm trying to avoid. The best I can get is WIC. It'll get me free milk, juice, cereal, and formula when the time comes. But tell me, how does that help me buy diapers? But at the same time, my family has always relied on the government, and that was something I never wanted to have to do. I wanted to go to college and get a good job so I wouldn't have to have anybody's help.

Why did things have to get so hard...?

Jessie

Wednesday, May 21, 2008
Dear Diary,

So, it's been a while, but I have a good excuse. I actually don't know what free time is. I've completely forgotten the feeling.

We had our Band concert Sunday. It went smooth as chunky peanut butter. Don't get me wrong, because the Band rocked, as usual. There were some rough patches where individual sections were concerned, but other than that, it was nice. Now me, on the other hand, I bombed. I played what I knew and winged the rest of it. I guess it sounded okay. You know one piece, I was sight-reading? Seriously. I lost the music for the Flute part (which, by the way, was in my bag the WHOLE time), so at the last minute, I had to grab oboe for this one piece. It was okay, but it wasn't a flute.

You know what was really hard? Walking off the stage and knowing that would be the last time I ever played for anyone. That would be my last performance with the people that I grew up with. That next year, there'll be some stupid freshman take my place, and they'll get to grace everyone with music (not that I think I can grace anyone when I make noise), and while the Band is playing Low Rider at the rival's game, I'm going to be home changing diapers and trying to keep my child from being terrorized by a maniac. Whoever said silence is golden was an idiot...

Speaking of idiots, my brother... Dad had to drive all the

way to Mayfield to play music for a measly paycheck that might get us through the next couple days, only to come home to Eric going, "I think I have a brain tumor. I need to go to the emergency room." At which point, I'm laughing, because this is a classic for him. I can't explain it to make it sound like I'm not evil, or you'd understand why I'm rolling on the floor laughing. This is the same kid who went to the doctor faking appendicitis, only to have the doctor tell him to poop more. This is the same kid who faked a broken toe, only to go to the doctor and be diagnosed with the worst case of stomach uGCers the medical books have recorded, diabetes, high blood pressure, high cholesterol, obese, and in serious danger of a heart attack or stroke. I can only imagine what's going to happen today. The doctor will tell him that he needs to get up off the couch and turn off the Playstation and do something. You know, before he dies. And my brother is one to fake a brain tumor one day, and have been magically cured by God the next. This happens a lot. I'm annoyed for my Dad who's going to have to spend every cent we had to live on for the next couple of days on gas to take him to the doctor.

    Four months pregnant today...

Jessie

Friday, May 30, 2008
Dear Diary,
    Graduation is over for yet another year. But unlike everyone else who will be relaxing a recuperating from a hard year, I'll be preparing for a baby. Not how I wanted to spend the summer of my senior year.

Jessie

Where My Ink Comes From

<u>Monday, June 2, 2008</u>
Dear Diary,
  I get to find out what I'm having Friday. I probably won't write until then. Mary and my grandmother want to go and watch the ultrasound. I hope it's better than the last one, because I couldn't make heads or tails out of it last time. Literately, I saw the stomach and thought it was two heads on the last one. That flared a panic, needless to say.
  When does the morning sickness end? Seriously.
Jessie

<u>Tuesday, June 3, 2008</u>
Dear Diary,
  I went to the health department this morning to apply for WIC. I swore I'd never smooch off the government, but a single mom with no income? I don't have a choice. Besides, Mom says it's fine as long as you're just using it to get from point A to point B. It'll mean formula and baby food for later, and that's all I really need it for. There's things like this that can help me pull this off. I just need to get out and find them.
  I'm something like 4 ½ months pregnant. This kid can't get here fast enough. I'm getting anxious. When I find out what I'm having this weekend, I can spend the last four long months picking out a name.
Jessie

Friday, June 6, 2008
Dear Diary,

    Mary picked me and Mamaw up a couple hours earlier, so before we went to the hospital, we stopped at a few yard sales. They were set up all over the place this morning. We stopped at only a couple, and then went on to the hospital. The nurse said to show up with a full bladder, and having a full bladder when you're pregnant is horrible, so we hurried. I've been getting my ultrasounds in a little office Madison has on the second floor, but this one was done in the Women's Center of the hospital.

    The nurse was nice. She looked around at the baby, the ovaries, various things, taking her sweet precious time while I'm lying on the table about to explode. She finally let me get off and go to the bathroom, and I got back on the table. She asked if I wanted to know what it was, and I told her I did, that's what we were all there for. So she put it up on the screen, got a snapshot, and asked, "What does that look like?" He had his hand down by it, which is just like a man.

    Mary said, "Well, he's got to have something to do for nine months."

    My dad couldn't go, so he said to call him when we found out. Apparently, everybody but me knew it was going to be a boy, so it was no surprise. So Mary said to tell him it was twins. He was silent for a moment, and then said, "No, it's not." I laughed, and we went on to some yard sales. Mary went crazy. He's got enough clothes to start out on. We got some bigger ones too, but most of it is newborn. Other stuff, she bought and said when he outgrows it, we can put it in my aunt's yard sale that she has every year, since baby stuff tends to sell really well, and buy him some new clothes. Can't argue with her there. After that, we went to a restaurant, and then on home.

    Morning sickness has gotten somewhat better. I'm moving up to soup now...

                                                      Jessie

Friday, June 27, 2008
Dear Diary,
    I have a tendency not to write too well in my journals over the summer. Without school drama, nothing's really going on. And if you just assume I'm worried or upset over something or another, there's really nothing to update.
    So far, it's been a normal pregnancy. I may speak too soon, though.
    21 weeks down, still an eternity to go.

                                                    Jessie

Monday, July 7, 2008
Dear Diary,
    I haven't had time to breathe. Things have gotten crazy the last week or so. I went to the doctor and found out that I have to come back every Monday now because of a shortening cervix, or something like that. I asked two different nurses to explain it to me, and I didn't understand it either time. All I know is I have to be strapped up to a monitor every week and have the baby's heartbeat checked and to see if I'm having contractions. I also have to take a heart medication that's supposed to keep me from having contractions. I didn't even know I was having them.
    I saw the doctor and was sent up for an ultrasound after that. The nurse that did the ultrasound called Dr. Madison, so I didn't get to see her to ask what was going on. All I know is I'm on bed rest to keep from going into early labor. After the ultrasound, I was taken to another room and hooked up to the monitor. The nurse in there, Clara, said I'd get to see her every Monday from now on. It might not be so bad, I guess. There's a

big flat-screen TV overhead, and Dr. Phil was on. The monitor just looks like a belt buckle that goes over my stomach to monitor the baby. And when he moves around, you can hear it. It's kind of cool.

23 weeks pregnant Tuesday. I know I'm not excited about my life changing forever. I'm ready for something, anything, because I feel like I'm a sitting target free for the taking. What am I supposed to be doing?

Jessie

<u>Saturday, July 12, 2008</u>
Dear Diary,

Just do me a favor, and shoot me. Put me out of my misery. I had to cut last night, so I did it on my leg to keep from getting caught. This house has been swelteringly hot all summer, so I've been avoiding my arms when at all possible to be able to wear short sleeves around the house. I was getting ready to go to Mary's house to watch some movies with her, and the first thing I did, knowing that Mamaw was sitting in the rocking chair right outside the bathroom, is waltz out in my underwear and a blouse. I actually forgot that the cuts were there! She went off on how I'd better not tell anyone, that social services would take my baby away. I don't care that I got caught. It's just that everyone thought I had stopped a long time ago, I had become so clever at hiding it. Now, they're going to be watching every single move I make. Privacy is history.

Jessie

Where My Ink Comes From

<u>Sunday, July 13, 2008</u>
Dear Diary,
   Y.T.C was supposed to kick off today. And I won't be there.

                   Jessie

<u>Wednesday, July 16, 2008</u>
Dear Diary,
   I was supposed to go to the doctor Monday, but I couldn't get in. I went today, and asked Dr. Madison what was exactly going on. Apparently, your cervix doesn't shorten until you're ready to go into labor. That's how I understood it. The pills are supposed to relax the muscles to keep my uterus from contracting. And I'm on bed rest. That's not going to happen, though. Hell will freeze over before Eric lends my dad any help at all. The yard has to be mowed, Mamaw wants the garbage picked up that's been accumulating outside, and I don't have time to stay in bed all day. I got them sick in the first place. I owe it to them, right?

                   Jessie

<u>Monday, July 21, 2008</u>
Dear Diary,
   Nobody has called from school – Taylor, Mandy, no one – to see if I'm okay. I haven't talked to them. Then again, I didn't tell anyone from school that I'm pregnant, either. It's no one's business, and I'd like to hide it as long as I can. I'm showing pretty bad, so going back to school is going to be bad enough. With maternity clothes, I can hide it better, but most maternity clothes now, you can tell they're maternity. Me and Mary are

supposed to go shopping today at some consignment shops, because I can't wear any of my clothes now. I have a few tops that I've bought, but I'm tired of doing laundry every other day. I've only one pair of maternity pants, so I just wear pajamas around the house. But hey, who wouldn't when she's pregnant?

Dr. Madison still has me on bed rest, and Mamaw and my dad are completely against my going back to school. I talked to Mom about it, and she said, "Of course they don't want you to go. You might actually make something out of your life." She's right, you know. My dad and Grandmother think that you can take a GED and live on minimum wage. And maybe some people don't care to just barely get by month to month, but I've lived that life. If I'm going to have to raise this baby, I have to have a job better than minimum wage, because it's just not going to cut it. Maybe I could have scraped by on my own, but not with two of us. Not now.

I've named my son. His name is Benjamin Cole; Cole after Dad's middle name, and Benjamin for the movie credits of some DVD my dad bought. The name came across the screen, and I liked the way it sounded. I hadn't considered it in a long time, but it's grown on me.

I could picture myself in a little apartment room with a baby in a playpen while I'm sitting at my desk studying for a midterm. I could see my Dad holding Little Benjamin up in the stands while I'm marching in the band. Now, I'm wondering if any of this is going to be possible. I can't get a job, and the closest daycare center, whether I could afford it or not, is in the next county, half an hour away. But if I do this program that my school guidance counselor told me about (which sounds way too much like a GED for comfort, because you legally drop out of school to enroll in a class that lasts just a few hours a day), then I could stay home and raise him. But then I couldn't go to college until I was 19, and we'll have to stay here even longer.

I've actually thought about asking Mary if I could stay

with her for a little while after Benjamin is born. If I told her the situation, she would understand. I really, really don't want him around the yelling.

Jessie

Monday, July 28, 2008
Dear Diary,
      I finally got my school supplies. It cost me $10 at Wal*Mart. And to add insult to injury, I got this 'Erma Brown' cashier who insisted that you had to be 18 to buy glue. So after asking me for ID (I was using a self check-out buy the way, which I'm convinced is God's idea of a joke), I told her I didn't have any. She said, "Are you 18?" No, I'm not 18. "Are you over 18?" If I was 18, I would have said I was 18. And I wouldn't have pulled out my ID anyway after her insolence. "Well, I'll have to take this." And she just took off with it, after she looked through my cart to see what else I had that she could take. I didn't want to tick her off, though. She was a few pounds shy of an elephant, and given I'm fat, she could have sat on me and killed me. Her thighs have separate addresses. I look like Barbie next to her.

      So I went to cancel my transaction after she went back to her post, and then she said, "You're not going to buy the rest of it?" And Jones's line came to my mind, and I wish I had had the courage to say it. "You'll pry the money from my cold dead hand!" But I didn't say it. I just said, "No, I'm not," as rudely as I possibly could. What was I going to do with it? Sniff it? My Dad still has Lortabs from his heart surgery; if I wanted to get high, I could do it without sniffing anything.

      As if that wasn't enough, we had to go to Krogers...

      I go in there with my little WIC card, get a cart and rush through the store with my Sonic smoothie in hand. I grabbed a couple gallons of milk, some juice, eggs, and cheese. I'm ready to go. This stupid cashier isn't. And after just having left Wal*Mart, I didn't really care. She just said, "Oh, we're not taking WIC cards right now."

Oh, really? "The sign on your door says you do."

"It sticks on the door. We can't take it down."

I didn't have anything to say to that. I was dumbfounded. So put a sign OVER it! It's not rocket science! Or some other sign halfway through the cereal aisle, "Hey, don't count on buying that with WIC." Then she proceeds to ask me if I'll be paying some other way. If I had any money at all on me at that time, I wouldn't have been using WIC. That was the point. And then she has the audacity to say to me, "Just go back through here and put it back. You don't have to go around."

I just said, "Sorry. I'm not doing that today." And I left. And I thought how proud my grandfather would be of me at that very moment... The same man that told the guy at the draft board to go fornicate himself on his mother's table.

And hey, it doesn't end there. Come in a couple of weeks, I get to do stupid everyday!

Jessie

Wednesday, July 30, 2008
Dear Diary,

Dad and Mamaw insisted on us going to my aunt's house while Eric got to stay home. I guess I'm lucky, in a sense. I'm not horrendously ill or in pain like most pregnant women, but I stay obnoxiously tired. And I just didn't want to go. But Mamaw thinks when my water breaks, if it even breaks before I go into labor, I'm just going to pop the kid out on the floor, and we won't get to the hospital. I can't convince her that that's not the case. So

Eric got to stay here while I got dragged all the way to White Plains about an hour and a half away. We got there sometime early this morning, just got back home, and it's almost midnight.

    I'm exhausted. When I go up there, I can't do anything but sit on the couch and watch them interact with each other. My aunt and uncle, my cousin (the one whose wife is pregnant), and my dad all play music. While they did that, I had to play with my cousin's three-year-old daughter. It's not that I don't like kids; I just don't want them around me because I don't know what to do with them. She wanted me to read her a story, and then play with her 'cube' thing, where you put blocks in the hole that matches the shape of the block. And then I had to color with her for an hour. She's in love with my aunt, so I was relieved when they finally stopped playing and she could take over for a while.

    But it just goes to show you, I can't even take care of a little kid who can, for a large part, take care of herself. How do I take care of a baby that has to depend on me for absolutely everything? And last I heard, babies take a lot more love than they give. I gave Caroline back when I was done with her. I don't think that's going to work with a baby. I use to take the batteries out of my Amazing Amy doll because I couldn't get her to shut up, or figure out what she wanted. I can't take the batteries out of a baby, and there's no off-switch. And there's no alarm to wake me up from this horrible nightmare...

                                                            Jessie

<u>Monday, August 4, 2008</u>
Dear Diary,

    I couldn't be happier! I can't believe it! Someone was CONCERNED about me! Actually, a lot of people were. I was on Facebook, and Jordan, Riley, Lauren, and Brooke were talking.

Riley wanted to know if anyone had talked to me, because I wasn't at GSA. And Jordan said, "Really? She wasn't at Y.T.C either. I hope nothing happened." And then Lauren started talking about how we use to talk a lot after the academy was over, and she really missed it. I mean, it's not that I want to worry people. I don't. But they WERE worried! About me! I didn't think they even remembered my name. I was going to call them to tell them I was okay, but I never got anyone. Riley was at the hospital with his grandmother, so he wasn't up to talking. No guys, not dead yet. Although I'm sure when I go back to school, death will sound like the better route.

      I'm really, really wishing I would have gone to Y.T.C. I knew GSA was out of the question. I had to fight my Dad to go to Owensboro last year, and especially with the whole being knocked-up-and-ready-to-go-into-labor-at-any-given-moment thing, I think a trip to Wal*Mart right now is out of the question. If I had even asked, he would have laughed in my face. When I told him I got accepted into GSA, all I got was a nod.

      I'll show him. You know what I'm doing tonight? I'm researching colleges. And I'm requesting applications for three. I decided in middle school that I was going to be a music teacher, and even though I'm not sure that's what I want to do now, I'm still going to college. I'm not going to escape this life with a baby on a high school diploma. As far as I'm concerned, college is mandatory now.

Jessie

<u>Wednesday, August 6, 2008</u>
Dear Diary,
      27 weeks pregnant today, or something like it. Next week, I'll be due for my 3D ultrasound. I saw pictures of one on

Where My Ink Comes From

TV one time, and they're really detailed. You can see exactly what the baby looks like.

    Everyone is griping at me about going back to school. Nobody wants me to go. All I've heard my grandmother say for the past three months is, "You can go get your GED and it's just as good as a high school diploma." Yeah, they tell you that, until you go to get a job with it, or apply for college. And you can, but if I'm competing with someone else who has a high school diploma, I'm losing. Mary keeps telling me I'm finishing school whether I like it or not, and I can make up my own mind about college when the time comes. I don't know why I can't go back; I'd do more at home than I would at school. Of course, with school driving me to the edge on some days, Benjamin might not handle the stress too well.

    I asked the doctor about going back to school at my last appointment. She said that since I wasn't contracting anymore, I was okay to go back. I guess this means I'm not even on bed rest anymore. I don't know why everyone thinks I can't do it. They probably figure I'll end up dropping out, all the same. I'm not going to do that. I need to do something to make sure me and my son are going to be okay, and if that means slaving away in a classroom and dragging myself to a university on days when I would rather pour salt into my eye than study for a midterm, then that's what I'll have to do.

    ...Maybe I'm just a smidge excited now. It's still shrouded by all the negative thoughts with how I think I'm going to make this work, but it's a start.

Jessie

Where My Ink Comes From

<u>Friday, August 8, 2008</u>
Dear Diary,
      I got my 3D ultrasound today! I tried to make it on a day where Mary could come, but the way she works, it's hard for her to ever get a day off. But Mamaw and Daddy went in and watched. I could see him, and he's really cute! He has my chin and my nose, poor kid. I don't know how he can look like me and be so beautiful. He looks like his father, too. A lot. I hope that doesn't mean I'll see his father every time I look at him. That's a horrible thought on my part. It wouldn't matter, I just... Well, I'd like to forget about it. Although I think it's going be hard to forget now...
      The way I feel now, I still don't believe I'm pregnant. I really don't think it's going to sink in until the doctor says to push. It's more like this is all happening to someone else, and I'm just watching from the sidelines. Like a really, really scary movie. It's like, "This is what's going to happen to you if you have sex!" I actually woke up last night, really sleepy and out of it, and I thought, why not just not have sex? Then I won't get pregnant. And it took me a moment to realize it doesn't work like that. I can't go back and change any of this. And because of me, someone is going to hurt because he didn't have a say in who he wanted his mother to be. He's stuck with me. He never got a say. And I'm angry with myself, trying to understand why I was so stupid, why I ever let this happen in the first place. He's not even here yet, and I feel like I've already hurt him more than any parent ever could hurt their child.
      Benjamin, I'm sorry. I really am. I know you didn't ask for this. It just looks like we've both been dealt a bad hand.
                                                                               Jessie

Where My Ink Comes From

<u>Monday, August 11, 2008</u>
Dear Diary,

I've tortured myself for three years with PLENTY of opportunities to drop out of school, and I never did because I didn't want to be like my brother, or have to struggle in life like my dad has. Sure, I'm irritated about all the changes the school has made, and for causing me to have to switch to standard diploma, but I'm almost there now. Here's the confusing part; I hate school and all its inhabitants with every ounce of my being (and trust me, there are a LOT of ounces in my being), yet I'm allowing myself to be coerced into staying on homebound.

It sounds wonderful, you know? A teacher swings by, crams 8 hours into only a few at best, and I write for the rest of the day, or watch *One Life to Live*. No school, no stupid people, I get to stay in bed and relax like everyone is begging me to do. And that's great, but pregnancy isn't a disease. I'm not dying. And besides that, the doctor told me that I was okay to go to school. Even when I asked her about the half day, she didn't say, "Are you crazy? You can't go to school!" She said, "You'll have to see the school counselor about it."

Here's where my suspicion comes in; my grandmother has griped and groaned from the start that there was no way I could go to school. I double-check with my doctor that I can go to school. Me and my dad went out on the boat (and if I can go out on a boat, I really think I'm okay to go to a little room and sit for an hour). So while I'm out, my grandmother is conveniently called by the doctor to be told that there's no way I can go to school, not in a million years, not even a walk in the park, and to pick up a paper from the school to take to the doctor to fill out so I can go on homebound. Is it just me, or does that just not sound right? By the way, this is the same lady that when the doctor compared my Dad's heart to a pacemaker, swore up and down and was in hysterics over him having to have a pacemaker. And when September 11th happened, said it was the British invasion. No, I don't believe it.

I'm going to the school to pick up the paper today, and I'm taking it to my doctor, but I can't guarantee that the school will ever see it again. Because I'm talking to my doctor, face to face, and finding out what's going on. Because when Mamaw says she talked to them, there had only been a three-day gap between that and the last time I was up there. And I just don't see how I could go from bad to horrible in just three days.

But on a different note, I went to church last night. I don't know what I'm really trying to get out of it when I go, honestly. Every other thing that comes out of the preacher's mouth, I have to question or find some argument to make in my head. Like the other day, he said that people aren't excited about the church anymore, that he hasn't seen a Baptist shout in a long time. Well, he said his problem right there in the sentence. Dude, we're Baptists. If you want to see some people shout, you're in the wrong church. I've been to a Pentecostal church, and all they do is scream. I thought their preacher was having a seizure. When I went, they had the ceiling fan on, and I was afraid somebody was going to get hurt. The lady sitting next to me asked me if I felt the spirit, and like the dense idiot I am, I said, "Ma'am, I'm Baptist." But my stupidity didn't make her lose her moment. I'm not sure a hose would have broken it up But that's when it hit me; that's why Baptists are so miserable, because they don't let themselves feel anything.

And you'll never see a fat Pentecostal preacher in your life. Or a fat Pentecost, for that matter. That's because their workout on Sunday made up for every Fried Ice Cream Blast and every Hershey Bar they've eaten during that last month. All I have to say is, if God comes back while a Pentecostal church is in session, we'll never hear Gabriel's trumpet over them.

I like when I can laugh. I need to do that more often...

Jessie

Where My Ink Comes From

<u>Tuesday, August 12, 2008</u>
Dear Diary,

      Well, I was wrong. Apparently in a matter of three days, I went from being okay to being bedridden, supposedly. I can't go to school, I can't go to the store, I can't go to the end of the lane...Newsflash: I'm not dying; I'm pregnant. No, I am, because home bound's going to kill me before this ever does. You want to know how bored I am? I bought a coloring book and crayons from the Dollar General. And then when that run dry, I bought three scratch papers, B'loonies, and an Mandy Show tape. As in, for VCR. I pulled out my Barbies from when I was five. No, home bound's going to kill me first. I hate school, but it would beat all of this. And this means I'm going to be home all the time now. Whether I'm in school or I'm home, there's going to be stress and I'm going to be upset over something or another. So it doesn't really matter where I am, does it?

      More than anything, I'm just sick of being sick, and tired of being tired. At the last visit to the hospital, I had to get a shot because apparently, I'm in a small minority – a very, very small minority (3%) – of people with an A negative blood type. So after doing blood work once already (and in case you don't know, I HATE needles, and pass out nearly every time I have to get one), they decided they had to do it again, just to make sure I really did have A negative blood. So that took two nurses to get me through – one to shoot me and another to hold my arm steady since I was shaking so bad. But before that, I broke down and cried. Not because I had to get poked (I'm 17, I'm not that pathetic just yet), but because I just want to be normal again. So far, everything that could have gone wrong with this whole thing has.

      So they do that, I wait for two hours, knowing I'm going to have to take that stupid shot. And that needle looked more like a screwdriver. I think it was. And all the nurses are either saying,

"This is just the beginning! You better start getting used to needles!" (which, let me tell you how much that calmed me down), or "This won't hurt." Never trust a doctor or nurse that says it won't hurt. Because they're right. It's not going to hurt them, just you. This 500 pound lady walks in with this screwdriver, assures me that it won't hurt, and I fainted. A nurse was patting my face, shaking me a little bit, when I slumped forward onto her. I finally got okay, and either those nurses are bold-faced liars, or this lady literately struck a nerve. Fire shot through my leg. For three days, it felt like someone had dipped the entire right side of my body in hairspray and let me dry without a shower. I was in bed for four days, sick beyond reason. And the paper they gave me on the shot said side effects were rare.

  So, let's backtrack a second: The fact that this is happening already makes me a statistic. I'm in a small minority of women who got pregnant on the pill. The fact that I'm on bed rest for this reason is odd. I have a blood type that only 3% of people have, and of those people, I'm in a less than 1% statistic that experiences side effects from the shot. And yet, this whole thing is nowhere near over.

Jessie

Wednesday, August 13, 2008
Dear Diary,
  ...I'm sitting on the couch watching *The Titanic*. And that's great, but this isn't how I wanted to spend the first day of my senior year...

  My homebound teacher came by today. We were leaving to go to the doctor. We didn't do anything. She just wanted to introduce herself. I think she said her name was Mrs. Thompson, or something, I don't remember. But she's coming this Tuesday morning. I didn't really say much to her. She talked to my dad and I just stood there with a basketball under my shirt looking stupid before she finally said, "So we're having a baby!" Yes, and I'm not proud. "Grandpa, are you excited?"

    Wrong question. So far, he says he's not going to be here, he doesn't want anything to do with him. I don't know if he's serious or not. He says he's going to be on the river in his boat, that he can't stand a crying baby. Mary says we won't prize him away. We'll see soon enough.

    The doctor's appointment went well. Nothing new. I was hooked back up on the monitor, like I am every week, and me and the nurse make fun of the stupid people on Dr. Phil. Mamaw's been going with me. She says she doesn't want me to go alone. I don't know what she thinks she's going to do, unless she just wants an excuse to watch the big screen TV. And her and the nurse, Clara, they talk about her grandson in Louisville, and how she's going to whip my baby everyday for worrying her so much. It could just be me, but Mamaw acts like since there's been a baby on the way, she's got a little more kick in her step. Maybe my getting pregnant was the best thing I could do for them.

                                                      Jessie

<u>Monday, August 18, 2008</u>
Dear Diary,

    Why? Why is my family so bent on keeping me out of school? Do they think I'm just free game to the other ignorant people there? Or are they afraid I might actually make something out of my feeble miserable existence? Which is it?

    Dr. Madison OKAYED me to go back to school. Gave me the paper to release me, said to take it to the school, and I could start back as soon as they got the paper. I was so happy, I was on cloud nine. I was going to go back and start my senior year. I ran out to the waiting room, thrilled out of my mind, and showed the paper to Mamaw. "Guess what? I can go back to school!"

You know what she said? She didn't say she was glad I was okay now, she didn't say she was happy that I could go back. She just said, "You look like going back to school. Look at you! Are you stupid?" Right in front of everyone. So besides being mortified, I was angry. She knows how important school is to me, even if I do hate it with a passion. And why she can't understand that... Well, it's not just her. We got back out to the car, and her and my dad got into it. "Billy, she doesn't need to go back to school!" And he AGREED! So, now I'm sure we're breaking some kind of law, because I'm supposed to go back to school. I'll just talk to the doctor next week and see if I can stay on homebound, as bad as I hate to.

If I wasn't so stupid, I wouldn't even be here. I would have downed some aspirin and it would all have been over with. Or let's do even better than that. Why did I let myself get pregnant? I know I'm stupid, but I didn't think I was ignorant, and I'm starting to think I am now. How stupid do you have to be? I knew better! I knew the pill wasn't 100%, I knew that! And I'm going to have to live with one stupid mistake the rest of my life because I got pregnant from it!

I shouldn't have even taken the test. I should have just downed the pills like I had planned, and I could have done it, because I never would have known about Benjamin.

Jessie

Monday, August 18, 2008
Dear Diary,

    As many scars as I have, a few more won't make a difference...

Jessie

Monday, August 25, 2008
Dear Diary,

    I had to go back to the health department today to get more WIC cards. I really need that formula. Actually, I was thinking about breastfeeding. It'd be better for him in the long run, and I never plan on having anymore kids, so I might as well give it a try. I can always go to formula if I just absolutely hate it. If nothing else, it's a lot cheaper.

    Over the last few months, I've been reading absolutely everything on pregnancy and childbirth I can possibly get my hands on. I've been reading *What to Expect When You're Expecting* like it's a bible. Magazines in the doctor's office, subscriptions to free magazines for new parents, everything. And I really like knowing exactly what's going on. Right now, Benjamin's lungs are pretty well developed. So if he were born now, he'd have a really good chance of living. And he's blinking, swallowing, and getting the hiccups. It's funny to feel when he does, because my stomach jumps in timed intervals.

    I've been playing a music box for him that someone gave my Dad when he had his heart surgery. I read that babies are so fussy because they miss being in the womb, so the best thing to do is imitate that feeling. My theory is that the music box will be familiar to him, so when I'm up with him at three in the morning, the music will hopefully put him to sleep.

    I'm almost afraid to say this, but I think it might have sunk in. Now when I say I'm pregnant, I think I really believe it.

Took me long enough. And I'm starting to think that I can maybe make this work. Maybe I can finish high school and, dare I say it, get a degree. And we would buy a little house out in the country, have a farm with lots of horses, and if we wanted to buy something, we wouldn't have to plan for months in advance. This might work. ...Or I might wake up and realize that I'm someone's mother...

Jessie

Tuesday, August 26, 2008
Dear Diary,

    You won't believe this! I actually saw the baby move! I mean, my stomach started flopping, and I looked down, and it looked like an alien was trying to pop out of my stomach. It was the coolest thing I've ever seen! I ran into the living room and Mamaw was sleeping in the chair. I started yelling and scared the life out of her. She thought something was wrong. I said, "No, look!" I laid down on the couch and pulled my shirt up, and he was flopping around everywhere. It looked like he was playing underwater jump-rope, he was moving so much. Mamaw was thrilled. Dad was off playing music at some nursing home, so he didn't get to see. But it was so cool!

    My teacher came by today, too. And it's Tamson, not Thompson. Melinda Tamson. She seemed really nice. She dropped off all my and went over some of the stuff my teachers wanted me to do. She seemed really surprised when I pulled out my school binder. She said she has to work with a lot of people who just goof off when they're on homebound, so having an organized student was refreshing. I think I'm a mass of organized chaos, but I didn't say anything. She didn't stay long, though. She has to see me twice every five days, so she's going to come on Tuesdays and Thursdays.

I'm afraid I'm behind, since I missed the first three days of school last week. There's not a lot of work, so I'm going to try to have it all finished before she comes back Thursday. I don't have anything better to do in the meantime. I'm supposed to work three hours a day, but I don't think it's going to take me that long.

Jessie

Thursday, August 28, 2008
Dear Diary,

    Mrs. Tamson came back today and was thrilled that I had everything done. But she said something about if she turned it in all at once, the teachers would think they weren't giving me enough work. I told her to take it all in and turn it in how she saw fit. But I'm done with school for the rest of the week, so that's one good thing about homebound. Well, I guess I'm cheating a little bit, too. I have Jones for two classes (Band and arts and humanities), and he won't send me anything, I know. I was hoping he would send a piece, or something, for me to practice on.

    I did a puzzle today. I did three of the 100 piece puzzles I use to play with when I was a kid. Well, I guess I still am a kid. And kids shouldn't be having babies.

Jessie

Tuesday, September 2, 2008
Dear Diary,

    My Lamaze class was today. I went with Mary, and I'm wishing now that I hadn't. It was really intimidating. All the women were there with their husbands, or even boyfriends. No, not me. Not that I don't appreciate Mary going, but it just shouldn't be this way. I had signed up for a couple more classes on breastfeeding and childbirth, but I don't think I'm going to go. The class was okay, just being a single mom in a room with a bunch of married pregnant couples is scary. I got a lot of nasty looks, like I was the only one who had sex. I wanted to scream, "I guess you're all a bunch of Virgin Marys, then!" I'll read a book on the subject. I'll get the same info.

  Anyway, Western Baptist is having a Childbirth Fair this Sunday, and Mary wants to go. She said we'd get a lot of free stuff, and let's face it, I could use some free baby stuff. I just hope it's not like that stupid class. If I get one dirty look, I'm gone.

  ...31 weeks pregnant...

Jessie

Sunday, September 7, 2008
Dear Diary,

  The fair at the hospital was nothing like I expected it to be! They had stands set up everywhere where you could get free samples of stuff, coupons for baby supplies, there were things that you could buy, drawings for door prizes, and the hospital was absolutely packed full of people. And I wasn't the only person there that didn't show up without a husband, thank God. There was one girl there that I know perfectly well was younger than me, and I saw a couple of girls I recognized from school that were pregnant, too. Well, that I had went to school with in previous years. I think I'm the only one at school right now pregnant. Anyway, with Mary there, we got twice as much stuff as I would have gotten going alone, so I've got bags of stuff to go through.

  After we left the hospital, we went to a restaurant, and we started talking about my grandmother. Mamaw wants to watch the baby while I'm at school, and she won't let me put him in daycare. And I know that if her sugar drops (she has diabetes, among other things) and my dad isn't there, Benjamin gets left with Eric. And that scares me. A lot.

Jessie

Monday, September 15, 2008
Dear Diary,
    I've done every puzzle in our closet. And trust me, there's a lot of puzzles in there.
    I've written short stories until I'm sick of them.
    All my school work is done.
    Ten more weeks of this misery.

Jessie

Thursday, September 18, 2008
Dear Diary,
    Mary said that after the baby's born, if I really wanted to, I could move in with her and finish school in her county. Mamaw wouldn't have a say in whether he was put in daycare or not. That would work, too! I mean, if it doesn't backfire on me. But I think it's a great idea. Dad will never listen to me, though. I told her she'd have to talk to him. And then when she surprises him with that, I'll beg him to tell me it's okay.
    I told Mrs. Tamson about it today. She said she thought it was a good idea, too. I think Mamaw's going to miss her coming around when I get off homebound, because she talks about her the whole week until she comes back. She use to desperately clean house before anyone came down, including her, but now she just lets it go. She says, "She can close her eyes if she doesn't want to look at the filth!" Our house is piled up with

junk, especially with trying to get a baby's room ready and get everything moved around. So our house is a mess. Well, it's always a mess, but point being, if my grandmother doesn't clean her house for you, she likes you. That's her way.

I'm rambling. I'm just bored, I guess.

Jessie

Monday, September 22, 2008
Dear Diary,

Mary found a crib at a yard sale that came with a changing table for $50, and I told her to grab it. If it wasn't for Mary, I don't know what I would have done. I've bought Benjamin a few outfits, and other people have given me diapers, clothes, some little things like that. Not that I don't need diapers. But Mary comes in here with three or four sacks of baby stuff every time she comes by. Or we go to her house, and she's got something for us to take home. She's got a stroller, a car seat, a bassinet, everything he could possibly need or ever want. I never could have done it. I owe her a lot.

I went to the doctor again today. Remember when I said that everything that could have gone wrong so far has? I was wrong. I finished that list this time around. My blood pressure has been up the last few visits, but Dr. Madison thought it was just nerves, I guess. Every time it would be a little high, she'd ask, "Are you happy to see me?" Once, I thought about saying, "Oh, I'm always happy to see you." I like her, I just don't like her needles. But she put me on some blood pressure medication, and I'm supposed to take it three times a day. I looked it up in my pregnancy bible," and she didn't come out and say it, but I think it's Preeclampsia; pregnancy-induced hypertension. It causes convulsions if untreated, and eventually death. She said the drug was safe, but I looked it up on the computer, and a website I found said that it can cause some problems with the baby. I trust her though, so I'm just going to take it and hope for the best.

Jessie

Tuesday, September 23, 2008
Dear Diary,

  When Tamson comes by, we don't get any work done. We talk about the baby and my future. Today, I showed her the baby's room, and the pile of unassembled crib in the corner. We tried to put it together and couldn't. She kept saying, "I don't want to cause you to go into labor, or anything. I can't deliver a baby." We started talking, and she's worried the father is going to give me a lot of trouble, or he's going to swing in one day wanting to see him. I told her he wouldn't, since he doesn't even want anybody to know that he IS the father. She wanted to know if it bothered me at all that Benjamin wasn't going to have a father.

  No, it's not going to bother me. Quite the opposite, really. I'm thrilled. I'm already afraid that he's going to have some of his father's personality traits, and that's scary. But if he's not around to rub off on him, that's wonderful. If I want my son to have a good life, the last person he needs is his father.

Jessie

Saturday, September 27, 2008
Dear Diary,
  I read a horrible story today. It's the one that inspired

that essay I'd written a long time ago, but it has more profound meaning now.

There was this woman who had six children, and said that she and her husband couldn't even afford birth control. Her husband had left her, and there wasn't anyone to care for her kids, so she couldn't work. All the government would give her was $71 a month. She lived in a shelter that charged $5 for rent, and she fed her kids with the rest of it. There was only one mattress, and the babies has peed and puked all over it several times, and the sheets had to be used for diapers. She had to wash dishes in ice cold water without soap that chapped her hands, because she couldn't afford to run the hot water. When the baby got diaper rash, she had to save for two months to buy a jar of petroleum jelly, but when she went to buy it, it had gone up 2 cents, so she couldn't afford it. She couldn't afford to turn on the lights or to buy candles, so they had to sit in the dark at night. The kids all had only one outfit that she would wash in cold water in the sink and pray that they would be dry in the morning before school.

She had a bad case of worms and had to be rushed to the hospital one night. The doctor told her that she needed worm medicine badly, and several shots. And she said she would just nod and listen, knowing that poverty meant there wasn't any money for worm medicine, or even time to be sick. She worried about how her younger kids would be so nutritionally deficient by the time they got in school and could get a free lunch. But one thing she said sticks out in my mind, and I can't stop thinking about it. Her oldest child was her daughter, and she said, "There is for her, at best, a life like mine."

Does that mean if I drop out of school and have to struggle from paycheck to paycheck, then that's the best Benjamin will ever be able to do with his life? I may not end up as bad as this woman, but neither is a life I want to live, and certainly not one I want my son to have to live. And if this is the case, then I'll have to go to college. I can't do that to him. He didn't ask for this, just like I didn't. We've both been given a rotten deal, but since he can't fight for himself, I'm going to have to do it for him.

Jessie

Monday, September 29, 2008
Dear Diary,

  I had to be put on another blood pressure medicine to take with this one. I'm afraid all of this is going to hurt the baby. I really hope the doctor knows what she's doing. She must know, because she said if my blood pressure was still up next week, she was going to have to take him. I don't know if that meant C-section or induction, but I don't like the sound of either one. I know he's coming sooner or later, why rush it? But I trust her. Besides, if it is Preeclampsia and I end up going into Eclampsia, I'm screwed. That'll be when I have convulsions, and could potentially die. But she's still never really said it's Preeclampsia, so it may not even be that. I guess we'll see next week.

  I'm back on bed rest, anyway. Why don't they just leave me on it? As soon as I'm off of it, I'm put back on, so just stop tugging me and leave me one way or another! I'm watching every tiny move I make, scared to death I'm going to make just the right move that's going to throw me into labor. That would be fun, wouldn't it?

  Well, he's got to come out sooner or later, anyway. What's the point in postponing the inevitable?

Jessie

Saturday, October 4, 2008
Dear Diary,
  I went to the Octoberfest parade our town has every year, and I saw my Band. And they were awesome! The freshman were easy to spot, since they all looked scared out of their minds, but that'll wear off by next year.
  I don't know why everyone tells me I haven't seen anything yet. Because everyone screams at home all the time, and sleep doesn't happen anyway. What difference is a baby going to make? At best, he'll keep me separate from everyone else. And when this is over, I'll be sleep deprived and miserable, but I won't be in pain. This is going to come as a shock, but I don't care too much for pain. Never have. At least when I go into labor, it'll be one horrendously unbearable agonizing pain for a few hours, and then it's over. And then I get to go live with Mary, assuming I still do that, and go back to school.
  Jordan said that his dad taught math at the high school in that county, and he says besides being a little dramatic, it's not a bad school. In case he didn't notice, my LIFE is a drama. I can handle that. But if I stay here, I'll end up quitting school, and seeing where a GED got everyone else, I wouldn't even bother. And hell will freeze over before I quit now. I've put up with too much from people for nearly four years, I wouldn't give them the satisfaction now. If I go to Lyon County, I can put him in daycare. And hell will also freeze before my grandmother will let me do that. I didn't want to do this, and they're not letting me do what I have to do, and my dad and Mary both already said it was okay. So try me. I couldn't get a job to support the both of us even if I did finish high school. I have to go to college.
                  Jessie

Where My Ink Comes From

Wednesday, October 22, 2008
Dear Diary,

I'm a mother.

Two days after my last entry, that Monday on the 6th, I went to the doctor for my weekly checkup and monitoring, figuring that even if she was going to go ahead and take the baby, I would get to come home first. I didn't even take my suitcase with me.

My blood pressure was 150-something over something, so Dr. Madison finally said enough was enough. I went into her office, and the conversation went exactly... "Your blood pressure was -----. What did I say I would have to do if I couldn't get it down?"

"...Yes... but by 'take,' did you mean by C-section, or induction?"

"Oh, inducing. No, I'm not cutting you open until I have a reason to. So lean back and let me see what I'm working with."

After a 'quick' examination (although I have to say, a visit with a gynecologist is never quick), she saw that I was two centimeters dilated. So I'm wheeled up to the birthing center, just in time to meet the girl that was 6 centimeters dilated, so I had to wait a while. (When my round at 6 came, I was more than happy to have given her my room.) I was finally put in room 3 to deliver, got into a gown, and was given oxytocin. Not oxycodon, the fun stuff; oxytocin induces labor. That wasn't working fast enough for my doctor, so she decided to break my water for me. To hell with mother nature, I guess. It didn't really hurt, but it made contractions get really bad, really fast.

The first contraction I felt, I didn't know it was a contraction. And then I had this wonderful thing called a 'back birth,' where the baby decides my spine is the most comfortable place to rest his tired little head. So I didn't make it past five centimeters before I was asking for my epidural with pride. Well, an hour went by, and they weren't there yet. And they were getting worse and closer together. I asked Mary to find out where the anesthesiologist was, and a nurse said he was prepping someone for a C-section. That prepping took another hour. I told her to ask again, and she wouldn't do it. I knew right off that it was a man, since he wasn't in a hurry. He finally got there two hours later. And every time I started heaving, he thought he was hurting me. The female nurse had to explain to that idiot that contractions HURT! Why did he think I wanted him there so bad? To look at that mile-long needle he was putting in my back? I've never cared less about a needle before in my life! It was so obvious he was a man.

And then, he couldn't get the epidural in. He got it in the first time, me telling him and the nurse both that nothing was happening. Nothing. So they finally believed me and got me back up to take it out and do it again. Three times, it took them three hours. The nurses had to take turns holding my shoulders. And I have to say, the pain was so bad, I don't remember too much about those three hours. It felt like the thirty minutes they promised to me. After the second failed attempt, the nurse said that because of the risk of infection, they had to quit after the first three tries. So I made sure the last time that I was doing exactly what he wanted me to do. You know why they couldn't get it in? Scoliosis. Apparently, I have it, and didn't even know it.

And there was finally sweet relief. It took the medicine longer to get to one side of my body, which sometimes happens. There were light contractions in my left leg for a while, and then nothing. Absolutely no pain. Even when I had to start pushing, nothing. Since I had the epidural, I was expecting a long labor. Nope. Twelve hours, and maybe fifteen minutes of pushing. And even as bad as the pain got, I still expected it to be a lot worse than it really was. Clara was on call that night, luckily. She took charge of the delivery until Madison could get there, and she said she didn't know too many people who could laugh during their own labor. The pushing was the hardest part, because it felt like I was pushing more in my face than anywhere else. And I couldn't breathe while I was pushing, so I got tired pretty fast. Mary and Mamaw were each holding a leg back for me, because I couldn't feel to do anything with them. Madison looked like somebody pulled her out of bed, and got there just in time to catch Benjamin coming out.

    5 pounds, 4 ounces, 18 1/2 inches long, born October 7th at 2:59 am, four days before my 18th birthday. He had a little trouble breathing, but otherwise perfect. And my grandmother got to cut the cord. After that, she was on cloud, like, 112, and when my Dad come in to see him, Mr. "I'm not going to have anything to do with it," and, "It's her baby, she can rock it," he was a few clouds ahead of her. He just kept saying, "He's something." He swears up and down that he looks just like him. And poor kid, he does, right down to his ugly toes. They're cute now, but this means when he's fifty, they're going to look like my Dad's toes. Gross. But he's adorable now, and I'll be dead when he's fifty, so who cares? Jones was right, though. Nothing changes a parent's stubbornness like a baby's face.

    So, baby's home, mom's home, it's over, right?

    Benjamin was a little jaundice when he left the hospital, so we had to take him back the next day to see the lactation consultant at the hospital to have it checked again. He had been under a light in the hospital, but it didn't get completely down. It was 12, so we had to take him back the next day to have it check again. It was 16.5. You know what it has to be before he can be admitted? 17. It'll cause brain damage in the twenties, and the way it had been jumping, I knew what was going to happen. I went home mad, and we called every doctor we knew. Mamaw finally called Bonnie from the Western Baptist helpline, who made sure he would be seen the next morning at the earliest time possible. And when we got there, sure enough, 21. And the nurse was like, "It's such a good thing you brought him in. We need to admit him right away." I was angry, to say the least. Not at the hospital, our insurance. We have medical cards, so we automatically have to wait until we're in the worst shape possible before we can get help. Just because we're broke off our asses, my son had to risk brain damage? Angry is putting it lightly.

The pediatrician said that if he couldn't get it down in the next three hours, he was going to have to be flown to another hospital and have a blood transfusion. But he said that he expected the light he was going to put him under would work, and just told us that so there wouldn't be any surprises. And it came down nicely. He was back home the next day, and everything was right with the world.

Oh, wait. Then I started having spinal headaches from that epidural everyone swore I should have. Dr. Madison said I needed a blood patch, or I would have to suck it up. Otherwise, caffeine can help, but it wouldn't fix it. Of course, I said no. I hate needles. That night, I had a fever of 102.2, and I was having chills. That on top of a headache that was worse than labor pains, saying it hurt is the understatement of the year. I called the next day, thinking they would just tell me to take some Tylenol and let it go. No, they wanted me in, right then. So I went, and when they took my temp, I didn't have to get weighed, get my blood pressure checked, or pee in a cup. I went ahead of everybody in the doctor's office. I was having pain in my stomach, too. It came and went, but it was severe when it came. Madison looked a little nervous, and said she was going to admit me because of my temp, that I probably had an infection. And I did, of course. It would have made things too easy if I hadn't had something horrendously wrong.

I was dehydrated. I had been too sick to eat anything (not that I couldn't lose some weight), so they couldn't get a vein. Again, of course not. They usually stick someone seven or eight times before calling someone else in, but the nurse said they made an exception for me because I was so hysterical. I reached a point in that hospital bed where I was abnormally angry at Benjamin's father and the world that any of this was happening, and I couldn't cope with that at all. When they still couldn't get one, they finally ended up giving me some valium, which is supposed to work miracles and make you not care about a thing. Didn't work. They ended up doing all the other tests I needed. They told me I was going downstairs for an MRI, and then back up to my room. A nurse had said something about a lumbar spinal, or something, but I didn't think they meant right away. They finished the MRI, and put me in another room to have that done. I begged them to let me do it later if they were going to make me, and they wouldn't listen. They just drugged me, and poked me I don't know how many times. Testing for meningitis. Yeah, I had that. Sorry, did I look like it? Was I turning black? I didn't think so. They wanted to make sure I didn't have an infection from the epidural, I think. I was drugged from the first day I was in there, I don't remember much.

    They ended up putting a central line in my neck. Madison insisted, and they all thought it would be best, since I was hysterical already. They had to numb my neck before shoving the garden hose into it. And when that stuff wore off, they had to knock me out. It felt like I was having a baby through my neck. It got to the point where they decided it wasn't the needles, and asked if I was suicidal. Yeah, that's it. I'm going to go into the bathroom and slit my wrist so that I don't get stuck again.

    After all this, an anesthesiologist came to see if I still wanted the blood patch. You know what that is? It's when they take your own blood and inject it into your spinal cord to repair the holes left from the epidural, the holes causing the headaches. I woke up to Madison sitting on my bed, asking if I still wanted it. I had slept on my head and had straight caffeine pumping through my central line all night to see if it would work. She said to stand up, walk around, and see what happened. It didn't help much, and I knew if I was going to take care of a baby, I was going to have to have it done. Until a nurse was like, "Those headaches will go away on their own, you know. It's not like you have to have this done." So after that, I sat and wondered why we were still debating this. Yeah, discharge me. Let's go home, screw the blood patch. I only had the can't-lift-your-head kind of headaches for a few days after that, and then they went from tolerable, mild, and then to nonexistent.

    So, we're both finally well enough that I can enjoy him now. I don't think he knows me, we've had to be apart so much. I still don't really feel like a mother, either because it hasn't sunk in yet, or he just doesn't feel like mine. At least he's easy to please. He wakes up, I change him first, nurse him, and he goes back to sleep for about three hours. I'm not really sleep deprived at all. Even at night, at least until I feel better, my grandmother feeds him a bottle and lets me sleep. I need to get back to school, though. I couldn't even tell you where I was in Spanish 2. I can't drop out this close to finishing just because I got too far behind to catch up and take care of a baby.

    I made it through this entire entry, and I haven't heard a cry out of him. That scares me a little bit. My luck must be pushed to the limit. I can't find the caps and nipples to all the bottles, his clothes are scattered everywhere, and he doesn't have any clean pajamas for tonight. But taking comfort in knowing that he's crying a little bit less each day, and he's gaining weight slowly but surely, maybe everything's going to work out.

                                                                   Jessie

<u>Thursday, October 23, 2008</u>
Dear Diary,
    I registered to vote today. When I went to the health department to pick up more WIC cards, they offered it to me, so I

went ahead and filled everything out. But if I get turned down, I'm not going to worry about it. I've more important things to worry about now, and it's not like Obama's going to lose, anyway.

Benjamin threw up everywhere earlier. Not spit up, I mean puked. He made pretty good distance. And my head is killing me. He started crying, and he kept on for two hours. I didn't know what was wrong with him. I had walked the floor with him, tried to nurse him, sang to him, and nothing helped. I just laid him on my bed and cupped my hands in my face. Diary, I had a horrible thought when I did that. I counted to ten to see if I would wake up and he'd be gone. I know that sounds horrible. I don't want him gone; I'm just wondering if the moment might come when I wake up, I'm a junior in high school again, and I call Mandy to tell her about the most realistic dream I've ever had. She would say, "Sounds like you had a night," or, "Did you eat something funny before bed?"

I would laugh and tell her no, but that it was alright. It was just a crazy dream, one that could never happen. "Imagine me a mom! I wouldn't have it!" I would say. "Kids are a far cry from my master plan." And we would begin talking about something else, just like that. I would forget about the dream in time.

Ben ran out of formula last night, and only had three bottles left until morning. We had to leave early and go find some before Mrs. Tamson got to my house for lessons. The grocery store didn't have any, and the drug store only had soy. Mandy's mom works there, and she stopped me to ask if I needed any help. I told her the situation, and she got some staff to call around to find him some. They finally found some at the health department, so we had to go back. Mandy's mom said they would have his formula ordered for me so much a month at the drugstore, and I could use my cards there.

You know how much that can would have cost me? $26,

and it wouldn't last him a week. The only reason the first can lasted him as long as it did was because when he was in the hospital and then when I went back in, the hospital provided it. I don't even have a job, just 'new baby' money from people that will eventually run out. I don't have to worry about clothes for him for a while, and he's good on diapers for what I HOPE will last him a long time. But when I get in college and I have to pay rent and buy books and groceries and gas for the car and pay bills,

...Never mind, he's crying again. That music box doesn't work the same miracle it did when he was born.

Jessie

Saturday, October 25, 2008
Dear Diary,

    My sanity is about to break. And the sad part is, I have a good baby. He doesn't cry until he's wet and hungry all at the same time. I'm the horrible mother that tries to blow him off with a pacifier while I'm too much asleep to realize he's hungry. He has to cry for a while before I know what's going on. And did you know I didn't change his diaper last night? Period? That's our routine; change, feed, sleep. I fed before I changed, and if I had changed him after I had fed him, the motions would have made him spit up, and then I would have had to make him another bottle, so I just laid him back in his bassinet. When I woke up this morning, I felt horrible.

    I don't remember the last time I played. I never thought I'd ever say that. Before, my lungs were just too cramped to breathe, let alone blow into a flute. Now, even when I do have a little time like now, I just plain don't want to. I kept telling everyone that single moms go to college all the time, and my mom did it, so there was no reason I couldn't. I was stupid. I'm too close to finishing high school to quit, but I don't see myself going to college now. I couldn't have paid for it, either way. And you know, I should be happy. Not only do I have a really pretty baby, I've got one that's not hard to please. Change his diaper, a bottle now and then, and he's in a coma. I'm not happy. I think when my Dad gets home, I'll see if I can just drive down to the river for a little while. Just take a break. Maybe write something. Short of what I've done on here, I haven't written in a while.

    It doesn't help that my Grandmother makes me feel like a child abuser. I know babies get cold easily, but at 100 degrees, I've got to cut him off. My grandmother freezes in summer, and insists that he needs flannel pajamas, a thick, heavy blanket, and then he needs to be held against me to transfer my body heat to him. Listen, there's such things as a baby getting too hot. The nurses in the hospital just wrapped him up in a little receiving blanket, and kept the room at 75. But I'm a horrible mother, I get it. And then she insists that she hold him and feed him and rock him, and then she gets on the phone and says all I want to do is play on the computer, that I'm not worried about him. The whole time, I'm telling her to let me have him, I've got him, I'll take him, leave him alone. "Oh, no, you just do what you want to do, I've got him." She's got him on the couch now, and she's holding him while he sleeps. He's got his yellow Tigger pajamas on, and his mouth is plopped open.

    Diary… I still don't feel anything. I don't feel like a mom.

Jessie

Sunday, October 26, 2008
Dear Diary,
    My grandmother finally gave up and took over Ben for a while. He started crying earlier, and I just started crying, too. I

kept telling him I didn't know what he wanted. I tried changing his diaper. It was wet, but he didn't stop crying. He wouldn't take a bottle, or let me nurse him. So I just held him and rocked him. I didn't know what else to do. My grandmother finally came back there and demanded him. She saw me crying, so she said to make a bottle, just an ounce. I did, and dropped the lid of his formula in some dirty dishwater. I rinsed it off and put it back on and took the bottle to Benjamin. I took him back to feed him while she talked to him. He looks at everyone else, but he won't look at me. I don't think he even knows who I am. He grabs my finger, but I read in my book that it was just a reflex, it doesn't mean anything. Mamaw said that he would know my voice from when I was pregnant with him, but all he heard was the yelling all the time. Some mother. I was horrible at it from the very beginning.

    Right now, I'm listening to my mp3 player. *Come to Jesus*. It's kind of pretty. Mandy said Blair used to play it in Band all the time on the piano, but I never heard it. Or maybe I don't recognize it from memory. I got started on a new song today, finally. It's called *Kiss Me Goodbye*. It's not finished, and I don't think it's going to be very good. It'll probably end up in the wastebasket with everything else I've written lately.

    You want the truth? Benjamin still doesn't feel like mine. He doesn't. He feels like someone else's baby. Like when you hear on the news about some kid being abused. You hurt for them, but you don't give it much thought once the story is over. I would never hurt him, ever, but that's how I feel about him. You would cry if a baby got hurt, but you wouldn't go to the funeral. I don't know what I'm trying to say. You love everybody, but there are people you don't want to go on vacation with. That's not it, either. He just doesn't feel like mine, let's leave it at that. When the nurse said to start pushing, I felt nothing. And when I saw him, I still didn't feel anything.

Jessie

Tuesday, October 28, 2008
Dear Diary,

  My fever came back today. I woke up with a pounding head, and to make matters worse, I was due for a check-up at the doctor's that day. When I called to make the appointment, the secretary said Dr. Madison had an emergency and wouldn't be in today. I was hoping everything was alright, but at the same time, her timing to not be in the office couldn't have been better. If I had gone in today, she might have slapped me back in the hospital, and I refuse to go through that again. So I had to suck it up and take Benjamin to the doctor to get his tongue clipped (that little thing under his tongue was too short), and he didn't even cry, poor kid. He's three weeks old, and he acts better than I do.

  I couldn't even hold him through most of the trip. I held him when I was sitting, but I was getting so dizzy, I was scared of falling with him when I stood up. I'm not eating anything. I can't bring myself to. It's not that I'm sick to my stomach; I just don't want to eat. I keep having this really bad pain in my stomach that started when I was pregnant, too. I thought it was the Braxton Hicks contractions I've heard so much about. Afterwards when they were still happening, I thought it was the infection. Now, I don't have an excuse. It hurts too bad to be all in my head. Mary said that a lot of women have problems with their gallbladder after they have a baby, but I'm too young to be having problems with that. I would hope so, anyway. I teased Ben and told him I didn't know if he was worth all this or not.

  I have to go back to the doctor Wednesday. I won't go if she's going to put me back in the hospital. And I'm sure she would if my fever was that high Wednesday. I've never had a 103° fever before. I was a little bit delirious, actually. Like, I knew my Dad had Benjamin, but I couldn't have told you where they were. And a couple times, I thought I was back in the hospital. 103° doesn't make you THAT delirious really, but it makes for some realistic dreams when you doze off repeatedly. It was 103.4° before it stopped. I had taken some Tylenol when we got home at about two o' clock, and it wasn't that high then. An hour later, I'm popping another one trying to get my fever down. My Dad laid Benjamin on my stomach and I finally went to sleep.

All I hear from my grandmother is, "You're going to get down," "You're old enough to know you've got to eat," "What's the baby going to do if you get down?" "You know what it's like to not have a mother," "You're going to die," "You'll keep screwing around until they put you back in the hospital." I don't know what she wants from me. I can't eat. I'm probably dehydrated again, but I try to drink all I can to keep from it. But eating makes the pain in my stomach surge. And besides that, like I said, I'm just not hungry. I can't keep anything down, anyway.

It's taken me two hours to get him to sleep tonight. He used to get a change, get a bottle, and fall asleep before it was all gone. Now he wants to stay awake all the time. He doesn't cry, he just looks around. And I don't know what to do with him. I was talking to Jamie on Facebook earlier, had him in my lap giving him a bottle and typing, and I was ignoring him. Do all parents do that from time to time, or am I just a horrible mother?

Honestly, I still don't even think he knows who I am. He doesn't know I'm his mother. I haven't done enough with him for him to know me. I've been in the hospital, he's been in there, I've been so sick everyone else has had to take care of him. We haven't spent any time together. And at this rate, he may not even get a chance...

Jessie

Friday, October 31, 2008
Dear Diary,
  Halloween has always been my favorite holiday. I like

the idea of being someone else for an entire day. I haven't dressed up or done anything special in years, though. At any rate, my Dad wanted to get Benjamin dressed up in his little Halloween outfit and take him trick-or-treating. We put him in his little pumpkin outfit, got him a candy bag, and went out for his first time trick-or-treating. Actually, that's a bold-faced lie. We didn't go trick-or-treating at all. Saying that we dressed him up and took him to various houses to show him off would be a better depiction.

    We didn't go to too many places. He's still too little to haul around like that. But hey, maybe he'll sleep better tonight, since we've worn him out. We went to Sue's and to her sister's and parents' house, and then to Mandy's. We tried to go by Jones's, but he wasn't home. I told Benjamin it was his loss anyway, since he was so cute. He didn't get any of his candy, though. After we left the first house and I got him back in his car seat, I set his candy bag in front of him, and he was asleep. I whispered to him and said, "Do you want your candy? 'Cause if you want it, I can get some somewhere else. Are you sure? Well, if you insist." He still doesn't know it's gone. I had a 50 calorie pack of Sugar Babies, chased it down with a diet Mountain Dew, and gave the rest to my dad.

    I don't know how I feel yet. I saw him out there today, and I just thought about all the holidays, what we could do. And I thought about when he would be old enough to take to the park and play, and I could read to him and tell him stories. And we'd be our own little family. And then I woke up.

                                                        Jessie

<u>Tuesday, November 4, 2008</u>
Dear Diary,
    He won. You know what's really sad is, I think Obama

was the better candidate for president. The only problem is, nobody's considered what's going to happen if or when he gets killed. And I'd rather have Bush another four years than have innocent people die just because someone thought that being white made them a better man than Obama.

    I can't sleep. Ever. We had visitors today (and why people won't just leave me and Ben alone, I'll never know), and one of them told Mamaw I looked bad. Well, yeah I look bad! Because people like you come over to see who the baby looks like and play name-that-father and won't let me sleep! Just leave us alone... There's a reason my son doesn't have a father, it's a good reason, and it's nobody's business but mine.

                                                                                      Jessie

Wednesday, November 5, 2008
Dear Diary,

    Dr. John said today that I would most likely have to have my gallbladder taken out, because 9 cases out of 10 of young mothers like me end up with problems with it. I was quick to give that idea the finger.

    I can't tell you how sick I am of doctors and hospitals and needles and pills and pills and more pills, "Take this heart medicine!" "You need this Prozac!" Yeah, when I went to Dr. Madison last time, she put me on Prozac. She seems to think I'm depressed. I wonder what on earth could've given her that idea... John said if I didn't have it taken out, it would only get worse. All I can say is, it's got to get a lot worse before I have mine taken out. And I've gone through childbirth, hint. I can take pain. I'm 18, so for once, my dad can't make me do a thing, including this surgery.

    Doctors always wanting to do something to me. I've got

tendonitis, "When your pregnancy is over, we're going to have to do surgery." I've got scoliosis, that's a new one. "I think it's time you had that back surgery you should have had years ago." Pain in the stomach? "Your gallbladder has got to come out." No! And hey... A bad gallbladder is awesome. It hurts like a cast iron bitch, but you can't eat much of anything, and who says I didn't need to lose some weight, anyway? They want to do blood tests and run scopes and ultrasounds, and I just don't see that happening anytime soon. I need a break before anyone cuts on me. And if nothing else, who's going to take care of Benjamin while I'm recovering?

    I haven't slept for two nights. I've grabbed an hour-long nap here and there, but I haven't slept. My milk supply is gone from eating so little, Benjamin's formula isn't agreeing with him, and he's always spitting up and fussy. Then he's gotten to where when he gets a bottle, he doesn't want to go back to sleep right away. His days and nights are mixed up, too. He just HAD to be born at 3 in the morning! But I just can't sleep, either. Even when he does sleep two or three hours at a time, I may not be able to hold my eyes open, I'm so tired. But when I lay down, I can't sleep. I think too much when I try to sleep. And then I can't relax. So much for Prozac.

    At least I go back to the doctor Wednesday. As much as I don't want to go, maybe Madison can give me something to help me sleep.

Jessie

Saturday, November 8, 2008
Dear Diary,
    It could have been a harder day. Benjamin only puked on me about a dozen times, and I got to sleep a long time, too. I laid

him up on my chest and he and I slept couple of hours. Mrs. Tamson just gave my work to my Dad and left. She had a cold and that was the last thing either one of us needs right now, particularly him. Because the thing is, when I go back to school, if he gets sick, I might as well be sick, 'cause I can't leave a sick baby at home.

      He's gone almost three hours without waking up. I know it can't last much longer. I know it sounds like I just dread having to even pick him up. And trust me, that's not the case. It's just very exhausting work. And since I've slept all day, I'm up for the night, and I hate pulling all-nighters. Well, it'll give me a chance to get caught up on some school work, anyway. Actually, that's a complete lie. I'm not behind in school at all. I'm WAY behind in Spanish. And if I have another worksheet packet in that stack that Tamson left, I'm slitting my wrist.

                                                                    Jessie

<u>Sunday, November 9, 2008</u>
Dear Diary,

      I'm so tired of not being able to sleep. No pun intended.

      I talked to Riley and Jordan earlier, too. They're both doing good. I told Jordan about Benjamin and how he's doing. He's stressed over school, but he's otherwise okay. And Riley's latest theatre production went well. They sold out. I'm missing all my YATA friends all of a sudden. I miss Riley and Brooke, Lauren, Jordan, all of them.

      I don't want to go back to school. I dread it so bad. Nothing is going to be the same. Everyone knows where to go, what to do, they know how to stay on the new principle, Durnham, and vice's good sides, and me? I don't even have a bell tone schedule. And why? Why couldn't I just go back with everyone else in August and learn and look like stupid with the rest of them? And while I'm at it, why do I have to be so scared of every little dumb thing? I'm so helpless.

    I have to go to Madison's again tomorrow. I've been having to pop three Tylenol PMs to go to sleep. I always have to take one more of everything or it doesn't work on me. I wonder how healthy that is on my heart? But anyway, I'm hoping she can give me something to help me sleep. If you couldn't already tell, the PMs aren't helping anymore, and the Prozac never did. I put Benjamin down a couple hours ago. He took a bottle, didn't spit up a bit of it, not so much as a wet burp, and went back off to sleep with the bottle still in his mouth. I love it when he keeps it simple.

    Jordan asked me if I knew how hard it was going to be going to college with a baby. I can't answer that. Of course I don't know, I've never done it before! All I know is, the best a high school diploma can get me is a minimum wage job, and that isn't going to support us both. So the way I see it, college isn't optional. My mom tried so hard to get me to tell who the father was. Yeah, so I can be talked into marriage, or what? Sure, let's get hitched. You know what though? It's like Mr. Jones said. Worse things have happened... I can't think of what any of them would be right now, but worse things have happened, I'm sure...

    Who am I kidding? I can't go back to school, I can't get a degree, I can't be a mom! When he was born, when they told me to start pushing, I wasn't excited. When he came out, I wasn't lifting my head frantically off the pillow to see what was screaming and what had been kicking my bladder around for nine months. Everyone kept telling me, "When you see him, you'll fall in love! He'll be the most precious thing you ever see! You'll know he was worth it!" I didn't feel any of that. When I held him the first time and I looked at him, all I thought was, "I'm screwed now." What kind of a mother looks at her child and thinks that? How can you look at your own flesh and being and think you shouldn't have backed out of the abortion? I hate myself! Because I do love him, but not like a mother should love her son. He feels more like a cousin or a nephew than my son. And I want to love him the way a mother should, but I just don't have those feelings because he doesn't feel like mine.

    I hate myself for feeling like this. Believe me, I do. But I can't work around it to actually feel like a mother. I know none of this is his fault. I know it's mine, the demons I'm fighting. But the other day, I was thinking about how he doesn't know anything about me. Me and him could take off and start a new life, and be our own little family. We wouldn't need anybody else. What am I trying to say? I don't know. It's like I've got a million things to say lately, but I can't put any of it into words. I've always been like that I guess, but now, I'm just losing it. I'm doing things that I haven't done for a long, long time. A long time. I'm not sleeping, obviously. I'm not eating, and I'm a little embarrassed to admit that I haven't written anything in weeks.

    I just don't know how to make everything work. I know where I want to be, and I know what's realistic. I don't know why I don't just drop out of school now and save myself the trouble. I keep telling myself I can't support him if I do that, but how do I expect to go to college, get a degree, work, and still find time to be the good mother that I have no potential to be?

    You know what I'm going to do? I'm going to go back and read ALL of my entries; all of them, and not just these. I'm going to go back and read all of my journals, all of my writings, all of my songs, and I'm going to find out exactly where I tripped up to deserve these past few years. This year, I got pregnant. Last year, I lost my best friend and I almost lost my dad. The year before that, Mom decided she's going to waltz right back into our lives and make up for lost times. And the year before that, and the year before that, and the year before that. You think I've had a hard year, Jordan? I've had a hard year for the past seven years! Because something has happened every year since I was eleven years old that has just... Sometimes, I get so down, a problem comes up, but my niche has always been that I've found a solution to every problem in my life, even if it was only temporary. And for once, I don't know how I'm going to get myself out of this. I don't know... What am I trying to say? I guess... Does anybody even care that I'm hurting at all?

Jessie

Thursday, November 27, 2008
Dear Diary,

  I was so excited about this Thanksgiving, and Christmas too. I haven't been for years, but I guess with Benjamin, getting a chance to show him off, I was looking forward to it. And for what? For someone to be rude to me and my son.

  I haven't cut my arms in ages, just my legs, so I could wear short-sleeves when I saw my mom. But before that, we had Thanksgiving dinner at my aunt's house, but I decided to go ahead and wear a mid-sleeve. I got Benjamin dressed up really cute to show him off, and my cousin has his new baby there, and everyone is having a good time. Until my cousin's aunt sees my arms and decides to ask me, "Are you still being stupid?" I didn't say anything. A couple minutes later, my Dad wanted to hold Benjamin. I teased him and said, "You see how that goes, Ben? I change you and feed you, and Papaw gets to play with you." And then she goes off saying, "Did you think it was going to be easy? Hold a nickel between your legs and that'll keep you from having anymore."

  If you're going to make fun of me, don't do it to my face. I'd rather not know, because I can't handle rejection. So I went home and cut in spite of it, this time on my arms. I told Mom about it later, and she agreed that that was uncalled for. So, my

Dad's side of the family thinks I'm the scum of the earth, and my Mom's side just doesn't care. Where does that leave me?

I'm dreading Christmas now. And I don't care of it's 1000 degrees outside, I'm never wearing short sleeves again. That way, I can get away with cutting when I actually do, since people would just assume I was hiding old scars. I got a newsflash for her; those scars are still going to be there in fifty years. Does having the scars make me stupid? I could remind her how stupid she was when her husband beat her up and killed her animals, and how stupid she was to stay with him. I could remind her of that, but I'm a nicer person than she is. But if I'm still stupid in fifty years, that means she'll still be stupid in fifty years, so who's the idiot now?

What really angers me is that everyone just assumes since I've had a baby, I'm the scum of the earth, that I'm a horrible person. Yeah, I must have slept with twenty guys, and not naming the father, I must not know who he is. I probably got drunk or high at a party and didn't even remember having sex. Is that what they think? Because if it is, they're more wrong than they know. I have a baby, and I'm automatically a bad person, is that it? One thing's for sure; people can make as many cracks at me as they want. I don't care anymore. My son is the only family I need, so I'm not going to fight for people who don't care about me. But if any of them think for a second that I'm going to take them making cracks at him just because of a little mistake that I made, they'd better think again. I won't have it.

People have been so good about everything, for the most part. I took Benjamin to church, and any other preacher would have just used me as an example. But he and the whole church weGComed me back. Both my aunts and uncles have fallen in love with him. Even Mom eventually stopped asking me who the father was and just accepted that I didn't want to name him and I wanted to do this alone. And most of the rest of my family has been really good about it, so I'm not going to talk bad about them just because of one stupid relative's ignorance. But my son is all I need, so as of now, I'm not going to put up with anyone who doesn't accept him, family or not.

...I just wish Gabriel's first Thanksgiving had been better...

Jessie

Monday, December 1, 2008
Dear Diary,

This is my last week with Tamson. I'm going to miss that lady. If nothing else, I know exactly what's going to happen when I go back to school. People are going to be completely ignorant and never let me have one moment of peace. I'm dreading it with a passion. I don't know how Mamaw thinks she's going to take care of Benjamin while I'm at school, but I don't know why she won't just let me put him in daycare, either. I wouldn't just drop him off somewhere, I'd check them out first. But there's not much school left. Maybe I can do it. I'll have to do it. My son won't make it if I don't.

Jessie

Thursday, December 4, 2008
Dear Diary,

Today was my last day with Tamson. She got some pictures of Benjamin and me, and swore she was going to come back and visit. Diary, Mrs. Tamson has never noticed my scars before today. I don't remember how we got into it exactly, but I mentioned them or made some kind of reference to them, and she said, "What do you mean 'scars?'" I looked at her like she had grown four heads. I had come to trust her enough to wear short sleeves around her if the house was too hot for a sweater, but I couldn't wrap my mind around her having never noticed before. There were too many scars not to have seen, yet she never had. So when she said that, I raised my arm and showed her. I've never put my arms up on display like that, but she seemed interested to know what I was talking about.

"I didn't know this about you, Jess."

We talked for a long time. I didn't give her much detail; just that I had depended on a blade for so long, how could I ever stop? Weary of the fact that she was still a teacher with legal obligation to report certain things, I bit my tongue when she kept asking questions. She finally told me to go back to school next week, and make two lives happen. She said, "You know as well as I do, you're too damn stubborn to quit."

I'll really miss her. I think I do already. Besides being a wonderful teacher, we've become friends. I think my whole family likes her. The very first day she pulled up, being as weary of authority as I am, I wanted her gone, mostly because I didn't know who she was. I never would have thought that the day would come that I didn't want her to leave. She calmed my fears when no one else could, and listened when no one else would. I owe her more than what I can ever pay.

Jessie

Monday, December 8, 2008
Dear Diary,
    I went to the doctor today with Mamaw. Not Madison, I

went to see Dr. John. I needed to get my scoliosis checked out before I go back to school tomorrow (for real, this time). Turns out it's pretty bad, but he said there wasn't anything he could do. So I just live with this pain in my back for the rest of my life? Genius. But Mamaw, bent on keeping me on homebound, asked him if there was anything he could put me on it for. He said no, and wanted to know why I wanted to stay on it. I said, "I don't. She does." So now that Mamaw is angry that I still have a chance to make something our of my life, tomorrow will be worth going back.

I spent the rest of the night getting my bag ready to go back. I didn't pack all my books, since I have something like a thousand to take back. At least, they have the weight of several thousand books. I'll take the books for the classes I care about, and take the rest in Wednesday. At least if I'm at school, I'm not at home with my brother. But does that make me a horrible mother to leave Benjamin there to fend for himself?

Jessie

Tuesday, December 9, 2008
Dear Diary,

I told Benjamin this morning before I left that it was going to be a good day. I didn't lie to him; he was going to have a GREAT day...

I didn't even step out of the car before people started staring. I made it in and didn't know where I was supposed to go. In one of my classes, a girl sitting behind me asked someone if I was the girl who was pregnant. I heard someone say, "My God, she looks like she had triplets!" Later, there was a stench out in the hallway, and someone asked what smelled. Some guy behind me said it must be after-birth. His friend, confused, said,

"Afterbirth?"

"Yeah. The slut over there just had a bastard." To make matters worse, he pointed me out for everyone who couldn't connect my face with my name.

At least they didn't say it to my face. I'd rather be talked about behind my back then have someone insult me to my face and me stand there and look stupid because I don't know what to say in my defense. My brother told me this morning I deserved whatever anyone dished out for me today, so I guess the whore will just have to shut up and take it. I deserve it, right? I got knocked up, and I chose to ditch my son and go back to school. And all that proves is that I'm well on my way to being just like my mother. That's my biggest fear. If I was any mother at all, I'd be at home with my son, but I'm so selfish, all I care about is me... And I justify it by reminding myself that I can't raise a baby on a minimum wage job, and that school is only logical.

I know people see me different now. I don't want to face anyone at school. It's too much. I know what they're thinking when they look at me. I'm so pathetic. Even teachers acted like I was one of those girls that cause a lot of trouble, and nobody seems to remember that I'm still the same old Jessie.

...That's my problem... I'm just the same old Jessie...

I don't see this working. I don't know what I'm going to do, because just hating school as much as I did was enough to make me want to quit, but I always found something to hang on to. Now, along with hating school with a sincere and burning passion, I hate being away from my son with a sincere and burning passion. You know I put his bootie in my bag just so I could take it out and look at it, and feel and smell him? I'm pathetic.

Blair said God would be listening. Where is He, Blair? I don't hear Him. I can't hear Him above the harsh words at school and the yelling at home.

...I don't know... I just don't know... I think I'm losing my mind...

Jessie

Wednesday, December 10, 2008
Dear Diary,

    I came back just in time for midterms. To be honest, I've been somewhat spoiled on homebound, and it might have been cheating anyway, but I miss the luxury of having the internet at my disposal. I didn't have to do anything, really. Even Spanish became a breeze when I found this wonderful, beautiful invention called the online translator. And if my homework doesn't get done at school, it doesn't get done. Not with Benjamin at home waiting on me. Everyone told me to prioritize, and I didn't give myself a chance to figure out why. I do homework during lunch, that's twenty minutes or so that I can work. I was late this morning, but if I get there early, I can sit and do homework in the gym. And I have a couple 'sleeping' classes where we do absolutely nothing. Even on tests, the teacher just reads us the answers the day before.

    Oh, our band concert is Friday. Got back just in time for that, too. That's nice. The music is fairly easy, though. It shouldn't take too much effort to make the pieces playable. Jones said I didn't have to do it, but I want to. I haven't played with them since May, after all. My dad has to play music somewhere Friday, and it's a $200 gig, so he can't miss. Marylou can take me, maybe.

    I only got called a whore twice today, too. It's been a better day...

Jessie

Friday, December 12, 2008
Dear Diary,
      The Christmas concert actually went really nice. My own abilities have much to be desired, but besides the point. Hey, Jones was right. I've only played the music for four days, and to only have that little time, I did okay. That has to say SOMETHING about my abilities, right? Right? Like, maybe I don't suck completely?

      Anyway, I took Benjamin to the concert with me. I didn't have much of a choice. Mary took us, and I tried to get her to hold him while we walked in. She said to hold him myself, and be proud of him. She wasn't the one who got the dirty looks. The Band people were fine with it, just like I knew they all would be. I only got one nasty smirk from a choir person, who didn't even have the audacity to do it to my face. I only saw her out of the corner of my eye, and I knew she was looking at me. I'm not stupid... Not that stupid...

      I'm sorry, but I'm starting to get the impression that this is the worst thing that has ever happened in my miserable little life. Jones said back in March that it wasn't, but I'm starting to think this is the first time he's ever been wrong. Some of these girls that are calling me a whore, I'm shocked haven't gotten themselves knocked up yet. And when they do, I won't be too surprised if they don't know who the father is. Benjamin's father doesn't have the right to breathe, and he will be blessed not to have him in his life. I don't need his money. I would rather raise my son sleeping under a bridge and playing flute on the sidewalk with my case open than have to put Benjamin through what he would go through to know his father.

      And I'm back to my inner battle... Nobility, or stupidity...

      Holly asked me about Benjamin's father today. She wasn't nosey, but I still just gave her the it's-way-too-complicated look, and went on. And my God, is it complicated... But anyway, besides one person's ignorance, the concert went okay. I even, dare I say it, played well. Well enough that when I hit a sour note, it was easy to blame the freshman for it. No one knew it was me but Jones.

      Jones held and kissed Benjamin, and I told him he'd be in his class someday. He's either going to play trumpet, or be the next Mozart. Or both. Or he may be just like his father, God forbid.

      Speaking of God, I still don't hear Him...

Jessie

Saturday, December 13, 2008
Dear Diary,

      I remember going to see Jones after I had tried to kill myself. He told me I needed to talk to God. I told him I didn't believe in God, that for there to be so much pain in the world, He must not exist. He went into his office and came back with a bunch of pictures from his last vacation. They were nature scenes, underwater, landscapes, and sunsets. I asked him what I was looking at, and he said, "You don't see that? That's how I know God exists."

      I wish I could have that faith.

Jessie

Saturday, December 13, 2008

Hey, Jessica. Glad to have you back at school. I hope you're enjoying being back.

I just wanted to thank you. It does my heart good to see the musings of an amazing writer such as yourself. Many of our cohorts simply cannot appreciate the profound power of the written word. It's truly evident that you can.

Please let me know if there's anything I can do to make your transition at school any easier...or if you just wanna talk.

I look forward to reading your book(s).

Postscript: Congrats with Benjamin...he's a cute baby!

      I don't think I've ever said two words to this guy. Daniel was in my chemistry and AP government class last year, but I don't think outside of, "What was our homework in here yesterday?" we've never spoken. But not having talked to anyone at school, I decided to message him back. I didn't feel like complaining, so I just said that ignorant people weren't being as bad as I thought they would be.

I think that's in the design of most people. They're ignorant. They're stupid. They're almost hopeless. But, sometimes they surprise you and rise above themselves. Don't lose faith in seeing someone be better than they are. It's real, I promise.

      "I just wanted to thank you. It does my heart good to see the musings of an amazing writer such as yourself," got me. Amazing writer? Sure...

Jessie

Where My Ink Comes From

Sunday, December 14, 2008
Dear Diary,

    Today, I listened to my mp3 player on full blast, the baby crying for, like, five minutes before I ever heard him (I thought my Dad was in there with him), while I laid on my bed writing dumb stuff to the music as I listened to it. *All around the country. Toast. Yeah, toast. Have a little jelly, have a little jam. Yeah, toast! Didn't know what would go... Milk and cereal. I keep them for myself. Cheerioioioioioios.* I look like one to listen to music about food.

    I dread going back to school Monday. I think going back either makes me incredibly mature, or incredibly stupid. I think it's getting a little bit better each day, but for the most part, I'm just going to have to take it until the day I graduate. Why not quit and get my GED? Because I would never give those morons at school the satisfaction. That, and it's just not as good as a high school diploma, and they only tell you they're equal until you go to use them. No, I'm going to make them put up with me until the end of the year...

    But you know, I don't care about them. I always say it's not mean if it's right, and they're right. That said, I really hate school more than before, if that's possible, because I have to leave my son at home. But if I quit, I'd have to get a job, and I'd still be away from him eight hours out of the day, if not more. So if I must spend the day away from him, I might as well be doing something productive.

                                                Jessie

Wednesday, December 17, 2008
Dear Diary,
> Yet more musings from a mediocre songwriter. The inspiration for this one lies with the eyes at school that are burning holes into my back...

Scarlet Letter

Another day goes by,
Another scar's been made,
I've come to hate the sun,
That starts the day again.
I can't see what I have,
Through the smoke of fires I've set.
I can't put out the flames,
That are still burning inside.

Pre-Chorus
I can't bring myself to pray,
I don't want to face the life I've made.
I can't tell You the truth,
I can't believe the truth myself.

Chorus
Father, can You read the words,
I've written in my heart,
That I'm afraid to say?
Do You know the secrets,
I can't tell anyone,
Out of fear of disbelief?
I come crawling back to You,
But I can't bring myself to speak.

Where My Ink Comes From

Will You read my scarlet letter,
And take me back again?

My diary is a lie,
My own expression false,
Nobody sees the tape,
I've stripped across my mouth.
I'm waiting for the day,
I can break my silent vow,
And let myself be known,
To the world that I've shut out.

Pre-Chorus
I'm ashamed for You to see,
The face for the life I have made.
I can't reveal the truth,
I have come to learn not to trust.

Chorus
Father, can You read the words,
I've written in my heart,
That I'm afraid to say?
Do You know the secrets,
I can't tell anyone,
Out of fear of disbelief?
I come crawling back to You,
But I can't bring myself to speak,
Will You read my scarlet letter,
And take me back again?

Bridge
Once again, I'm calling out to You,
I'm begging You again,
For Your saving grace,

Where My Ink Comes From

Hoping You will read,
The words I cannot say,
That nobody has heard,
Can You read me, Father?
Will You understand?

<u>Chorus</u>
Father, can You read the words,
I've written in my heart,
That I'm afraid to say?
Do You know the secrets,
I can't tell anyone,
Out of fear of disbelief?
I come crawling back to You,
But I can't bring myself to speak,
Will You read my scarlet letter,
And take me back again?

Will You forgive me?
Will You forgive me?

Read my scarlet letter,
Please take me back again.

Take me back,
Take me back again.

    It's a beautiful song. I think so, anyway, and it means something if I'm saying it. I just wish that I actually could be taken back. But look at me... Satan wouldn't have me.
    I sent the song to Daniel, anyway. He told me that I could send him anything, that he wanted to read. No one else reads my music, so I thought… why not? I barely know the guy, and it's not like there's anything to ruin. He read it and messaged

me on facebook. He said...

Don't sweat the scarlet letter thing. The measure of a man cannot be determined simply by looking at the outside, but instead of what's written on the heart. My philosophy is to focus on writing something meaningful on my heart: I'm currently working on engraving "Proven Character." Forget about my naysayers...they won't be with me on Judgment Day.

  Not quite what I was expecting, but I'll take it! I've not spoken with him enough to know what he's really like, but if our facebook messages and IMs reflect him at all, he's a decent human being. Those are hard to come by anymore.
Jessie

Thursday, December 25, 2008
Dear Diary,
  Benjamin got $50 from his great grandpa, Mom got him a stroller, her partner got him two Baby Einstein DVDs, and my little brother (half brother) got him a storybook. Of course, everyone in a fifty-mile radius knows I got a camera, because I'm camera happy, and I have a picture of everyone.
  I know he doesn't care right now, and doesn't even know it's Christmas. But next year when he's big enough to get excited, it'll be a lot of fun. Maybe by then, I'll feel like a mom. In the meantime, I'm glad his first Christmas was better than his first Thanksgiving.
Jessie

Sunday, December 28, 2008
Dear Diary,
    When Benjamin is crying and won't take his bottle, I don't know if he's gassy, or fighting sleep, or if he's just gotten so hungry, it's made him so mad and frantic, he doesn't realize he's got the bottle in his mouth. And then I'm thinking, "Well, if that's the case, I must be pretty horrible for letting him get that hungry."
    I've been staying up all night and catching catnaps throughout the day. I can't sleep at night, and when I'm horrendously exhausted and go to lay down, it's a quick doze, snap back up, and I'm wide awake. I'm been doing this for three weeks. For three weeks now, I've been living on coffee and the drive to continue.
    If I could only use one adjective to describe myself, no other words, and I only had three seconds to come up with the word, let's see... lost. Completely lost. I'm going around and around, and I'm completely confused and not sure where I'm trying to go, or what I'm trying to say. You know how you wake up at night and you're still half asleep, so you can't think straight? I live in that right now.
    Diary, help. You listen. No one else does, but you do. And I need help.

                                                Jessie

Friday, January 2, 2009
Dear Diary,
    I was up all night last night again. Benjamin just did NOT want to cooperate with authority. Well, it wasn't his fault. He has a cold. He's still stuffy, and he couldn't breathe through his nose and take his bottle at the same time, and it ticked him

off. So he'd finally give up and go to sleep hungry, and I felt so sorry for him. But because he went to sleep hungry, he'd only sleep about an hour or less. So I might have a couple of hours of sleep under my belt, I'm not too sure. He couldn't get down more than an ounce or two at a time, but he didn't starve, at least.

I've a lot of work to do from now until I go back to school. I still have work to make up, and I have to study for five different finals. I have to go back in three days.

...And why I'm even going back...

The baby is asleep in my lap. He's too cute. He's got his I Love Mommy bib on, and overalls, and babies always look cute in overalls.

Why can't I be better to him than this?

Jessie

<u>Saturday, January 3, 2009</u>
Dear Diary,

I've been sending more of my music for Daniel to read. I haven't been able to share it with anyone else. After reading one, he told me that only on the darkest of nights can you really see the stars. And if this is really as bad as it gets and as dark as it can possibly be, why can't I see so much as a shimmer?

You know what, though? I've already got secrets I'm taking to my grave. And I'm only 18! That means that I may have another good fifty or sixty years to stack up some more marks against me. And where's the line I keep from crossing that's going to make God just go, "Nope. Sorry, but you had your chance." I think I've already crossed it, anyway.

Jessie

Where My Ink Comes From

<u>Saturday, January 3, 2009</u>
Dear Diary,
      I've been given a good idea. Daniel says that I should write a book for my eyes only, so to speak. Tell the truth, knowing that no one will read it but me. I've considered doing that before, but I kept thinking that there are too many more bad memories to be made. My life to the point is only one chapter of so many more bad experiences. I try to hear what he's saying, but it's just not enough for someone to say, "Things get better." They do get better, I know. But the people who say that have had all their problems resolved. When will my time come? Or worse, am I never meant to have it? Besides, I've lost a lot of those memories, too. Sometimes, I'll try to remember them, and I can't decide if they really happened, or if they were just writing ideas. But I think I did that on purpose. I don't want to remember those things. I told myself they never happened, to the point that I don't know the difference between my own mind and reality.
      You want to know the real kick? I want to. I want to gather up all those memories and all that guilt and fear that I've been chained to, acknowledge that all of it happened, so I can move on and forget about everything. How can I be expected to build a better future for me and my son when I'm too caught up in what happened way back when? But every time I try, I get too caught up in thinking that even when I forget, others remember. And nobody is ever going to see me as a writer or a musician, or anything worthy of being titled. Instead, they can't see past the scars on my arms, or my own ignorance in the written language.
      Or maybe it's better than I don't remember. One day, me and my son can pack up and get out of here as fast as we can go, and forget about everyone here, and everything that's happened. We'll be able to start all over again. I won't have to worry about old memories, because nobody would know us, and we could

make new ones. And I'd never tell anyone about anything. I wouldn't even write it. I'd just start again. I wouldn't have to live in fear of my son's father making himself known, I wouldn't have to wonder when I'm going to go too deep with a blade, and we could just be our own little family. I've always wanted one, anyway. And Benjamin would never have to know how horrible life could have been, or was.

      He deserves so much better than this. He deserves a better mother. And why I can't give that to him... Well, he didn't deserve to be born like this, anyway. There are couples out there that can't have kids at all, and women that would make a better single mother than I would. And Benjamin is a blessing to everyone who knows him. He would have made deserving parents proud. I know I don't deserve him.

      I have a million things to say. They're all running through my mind, and I can't get them out... I know God makes mistakes. Why else am I here?...

                                                                         Jessie

<u>Sunday, January 4, 2009</u>
Dear Diary,

      I write at school, and that's all I do. Even when I don't have anything to write, I just sit and write lyrics to songs I already know and love, thinking that maybe I can feel the emotion that that artist was trying to portray and weave it into my own creation; plagiarism without the plagiarism, so to speak. And every once in a while, I even manage to write a fraction of the truth. I write more than Stephen King did in his younger days. So, here's my question: How long do I have to wait before I write something worth reading?

      Writing music for me has become like an addiction to

meth; The euphoria from writing a song, or anything for that matter, you think is good is the most wonderful feeling in the world. And then that high is followed by a huge crash, after you come to that harsh reality that what you've written is just wasted ink and thought. So, here are my New Year's Resolutions: 1) Find out why I still continue with my music and my writing, knowing it's never going to amount to anything. 2) Find out what I need to do to upgrade from a mediocre status to at least an amateur status. And 3), Look for a hobby that has more realistic outcomes.

Let's throw in 4), to learn how to stop being such a downer all the time...

No, wait. As long as I'm in this whole self-pity thing, I'm going to go ahead and get this out. I know exactly why I'm a downer. You know, I got started in this vicious cycle of lose someone, be depressed, meet someone, be happy again, lose that person, be depressed until I meet someone new. And you can only go through that so many times before you've had all you can take. I'm better off as a loner. Don't take chances, don't get hurt. It's always worked. I have to sit alone all the time at school, and no one acknowledges my existence, so I don't have the chance to ever wonder what could have been. Every other year, I've just gone to the library during flex and sat at a computer, or I'd sit at a table and act like I was busy writing so nobody would talk to me. This year, everyone has to go to lunch, and it really sucks to sit there looking around at everyone and feeling sorry for myself. So I write to avoid the looks, and to keep myself from looking at anybody else. I've had people sit next to me a few times. And I hate when that happens, because it's usually somebody I've only had a few conversations with that wants to find out straight from the horse's mouth what the real rumors are about me. So I sit there looking stupid, because I'm so much of a pushover, I can't even tell them to go away.

But why am I like that? For lack of a better way to put it, I'm just socially retarded. I know why I feel so down all the time, but I don't know where I lost the opportunity to learn to speak, because I never could. I take the term 'shy' to a whole other level, to the point where it's ridiculous. I guess I'm just so afraid of people, I'd rather be a spectator than a participator.

That can be resolution 5: Stop being a mute...

Looking back over this entry, that's another thing I wonder about. As much as I write, what is it exactly that I'm trying to say? Am I really so lost, so crazy, so out of my mind that I can ramble notebooks and journals full of information, and never say anything at all? I guess it's like school; I hate it with a passion, I know I could quit anytime I wanted to and never have to face stupid people again, and yet, I keep going back. No, I guess there is a difference. Benjamin can do without my wasting my time writing nothing but mediocre musings, and we could both use a degree.

Remember when I said that I was going to go back and look at everything I had ever written, and try to figure out when my life went off the deep end? Well, I did. And you know what I found out? That I'm more screwed up than even I realize.

It's the same thing with my music. I thought hours of practicing would be enough. But I'm starting to think that it was only by the grace of God that GSA accepted me, because I don't know what I'm trying to achieve in playing anything. Jones tells us to portray our emotion through our music. My problem is, I can't even pretend to be happy long enough to make a piece sound joyful, and I'm afraid to pull up the memories that are going to make a piece sound sorrowful. I know if I do, they're stuck with me for the rest of the day. I can't bring myself to do it.

I guess I'm more or less on autopilot. I don't allow myself to feel anything, so I don't have to relive anything about my past that I've come to regret. I don't think I'm ever going to get past those things if I don't face them head on. But when I'm too afraid to even think about them, when I hate myself so much for the things that have happened, and when I can't even tell the difference between what really happened and what might have been a dream or a new idea for a story, what's the point in even trying? I think that's why I keep so many journals and notebooks. That way, I can write down only the days I want to remember, and if something bad happens, I don't write about it. I just go on, and act like it never even happened. That's probably where I screwed up.

But really, is that so bad? You don't have to remember anything you don't want to. Write about the good things, like inaugural parades, going to a summer academy, getting accepted into GSA. Don't write about going and sitting in a bathroom stall at lunch just to avoid the staring. Good memories, good life, good death when the time comes to reminisce. Nobody has to know anything about me that I don't want them to know. If I don't write it, nobody sees it, nobody knows. And that leaves me to myself, and I don't have to be anybody's burden.

So much rambling... And I'm not saying a thing...

                       Jessie

Tuesday, January 6, 2009
Dear Diary,

Here's my deal: I'm not big on poetry. Love reading it, love critiquing it, HATE writing it. My philosophy on poetry is that unless you're just an exceptional writer, and I mean in-the-league-with-Shakespeare exceptional, any poetry you write is going to... well, suck. And I'm not completely right. I've read poetry by Jones that has been remarkable, and someone from my biology class last year is amazing. It's just not for me. When you can't write stories, you write poetry. And when you can't write anything at all, you're a songwriter.

Anyway, here...

Natural Sin

Imagine your child has a tear,
You can never wipe away,
And it's a part of him,
Because you put it there.
He will ask you why it lingers,
And all you do is stutter,
You tell him it's not his fault,
But that it's all your own.
To a child, his mother is a god,
So he will be confused,
Mothers aren't allowed to make mistakes,
Perfection is all that's acceptable.
He will ask why God chose him,
And how such things can happen,
When God is supposed to be love,
And all his mother knows.
You will tell him you don't know,
Just how mysterious God can be,
Or the plan He has in mind.
Tell your child of the young pup,
Born of a dog and a wolverine,
Who does not have to act upon,
The bad blood in its veins.
He still will not understand,
And he will keep asking why,
Until you let him in on the joke.
Only with a heavy heart,
Do you tell him it's all true,
There's no smiles, no laughing,
Every word is so,

Where My Ink Comes From

To think you're dreaming is a lie.
How you wish you could be,
To shield him from the truth!
But it will not erase the pain he feels,
For such innocence lost.
You will cry for his impurity,
That he cannot control,
He will cry for the scars,
He knows lay on your heart.
The fear will engulf his mind,
What if people find out?
What if his past returns?
What if he must pay for your sin?
And you, like him, will become afraid,
Of what is going through his mind.
Will he hate you?
Will he forgive you?
Will he blame his incurable sin on you?
He will not forget the truth,
But of course, neither will you,
And every time you see your child,
You'll see the tear you've placed.
So place your hands inside your pockets,
Put your handkerchief away.
The tear you've left in your child's eye,
Is one that's there to stay.

              Jessie

<u>Wednesday, January 7, 2009</u>
Dear Diary,
   If you want the honest-to-God truth, Benjamin has me

more spoiled than we have him. He never cries, and when he does cry, you always know what he wants. Feed him, change him, he'll play for a little while, and then he takes a nap. He keeps it simple, I keep it simple. Well, that wasn't good enough tonight. I know I've walked this floor a good mile or more with him. My Dad has got him spoiled to it, and even if he's not here, he expects it to be made possible via Mom. And hint, Mom can't carry anything for very long without her back getting a horrendous stabbing pain. So by hour three of nonstop crying, I was stressed, to say the very least. And it wasn't even so much the sound of him crying, it was not knowing what he wanted.

I'm having a hard enough time trying to get into this 'mom' status, because I'm still not feeling much like one. Actually, I don't feel like one at all. I feel lousy. A mother is supposed to know what her baby wants, right? So why don't I? No, I know exactly why. It's because I insist on graduating from that infernal hell known as public high school, and I don't have the time to go home and be a mother. How horrible am I? And I blow it off by saying, "I NEED a diploma," "I NEED a good job," "I want this, that, all of those, and some of these." But does it really matter if he has fashions right out of the magazines, or if he has all the brand-name products? Should anybody really have everything they want without limit? And what does it matter what kind of material life I give him if I'm so busy working, I'm not there to teach him the life lessons and morals that he needs to function and be productive in a normal society?

Of course. What am I thinking? I know what goes on in my own mind, how I think and feel. What position am I in to try to teach anyone else what they need to know in life? I hear all the words, "Things get better," and, "There are people who care." I've heard it. I've been blessed to have Daniel's encouragement lately, and I've taken in every word he's said. I've listened to everything Jones has said, too. Even Jamie has tried to tell me that I need to let people in more. But the problem is, I only believe what I hear for a moment. Just a moment. And then, using my horrible logic, I find a way to contradict what they say in some form or another. Even now as I write, I'm thinking, "No one is acknowledging me. And those who do are just thinking how stupid I am. People who say they care don't, and I'm not going to be tricked. But Jess, you know you're wrong, right? No, I'm pretty sure I'm right." And the only reason I keep writing is just hoping that I'm going to someday be able to tell myself that I'm wrong, people do care, and I've been really stupid to think different. I think, maybe my time will come when, like Daniel, Blair, and Jamie, I can look back on these times, tell my story to someone else, and know that things are going to be forever different. But how do you look forward and build a better future, when you're still trying to erase the past?

So, I'm brought back to my internal battle. Do I continue life how it is now, or do I look for another way? Is there another way? Or am I just always going to be the stupid mute in the back of the room? I wish people could see past me and see who I am. But then what good would it do? I'd still be completely lost.

So, here are two sides to my status at school: On one side, I know what people think of me. And knowing what people think of me, I wouldn't want to have anything to do with me, either. On the other side, I think that the majority of people are ignorant, and for lack of a better way to put it, I'm one of the handful who have a grain of common sense. Then I go back to the other side, where I don't have any common sense. I'm a moron. I can't even say what I mean most of the time, and I get tongue-tied, and finally just look down to make myself shut up. "Stop, they already think you're stupid." Then I switch back, and decide that one day, I'm going to leave them in the dust, and they're going to wish things were different. Then back to the first side, where I'm an idiot, and people as dumb as me don't get to excel. That's where it ends. I stay on that side, because I've contradicted every positive thought I've had, and I don't have anything else to offer myself.

Jessie

Thursday, January 8, 2009
Dear Diary,
    We had this beautiful thing called a 'midterm' in tech math, my third period class. And I was so excited going in there. I had it set in my mind that I could do it, and I was going to. Tech math has been, by far, the easiest and least stressful math class I've taken since... well, since I began my high school journey. So I didn't even study for it. I figure the math is so easy, and the teacher gave us all the notes we'd need, and nothing else, to use during the test. So I had my caGCulator, and I'm sitting there zipping through them, a little proud of myself. Well, zipping didn't last to three. The notes weren't helping at all. I didn't know a third of those questions, the answer kept coming out wrong. And normally, I'd just let it go, and take comfort in thinking I'd do better next time, and I'd be more prepared. This is 50% of our grade, so there was no letting it go. I didn't even finish the test.
    Fifth is also my lunch period, so I'm making my way down to the cafeteria, notebook and mp3 in hand, only to find that some girls have gotten to my booth first. I mean, it wasn't the booth. I didn't care where I sat. The problem was, I didn't know anybody in there, and nobody wanted me to sit next to them, anyway. So I ran into some girl who wanted to stand there and talk, and I made some lame excuse about forgetting something in the room. I went back and dropped my notebook off, figuring wherever I went, I wasn't going to get to write anything.
    There was a meeting going on the library, so that was off. First, I went to the bathroom in the math hall, but a group of smokers made their way in there, so I left. Then, I went to the

bathroom up the ramp. No one was in there, so I want into the big stall and just stood there for a few minutes, realizing how pathetic I was. I was more embarrassed to stand in the cafeteria looking stupid while trying to find someone I might have slightly known, than I was to be caught hauled up in a bathroom stall. I mean honestly, what was I going to say if someone found me? So I got myself into this little state, and then luck would have it, I worked myself into a panic attack. Not a severe one, mind you, but enough that it got me even more upset, so I started having trouble breathing. My heart felt like it was going to stop, I was sweating, and I couldn't stop shaking. And trying to have a quiet panic attack isn't the easiest thing to do. So I tried to catch my breath, and once I did, headed straight to the nurse's office; NOT how I intended to meet our school's new nurse.

    She listened to my heart and checked my blood pressure. And she said exactly what I knew she was going to say. "Everything looks good, you can go back to class. Sounds like you just had a slight panic or anxiety attack." Well, I could have told her that. Way to state the obvious there, Einstein. So I made my pathetic little way back to Spanish, got a pitiful look from the teacher, like, "I know what's going on," and feeling like doing anything except finish that stupid midterm, I got back to work.

    My psychology teacher, Mr. Carson, asked me after class how my day was. And I knew what I was supposed to say, I just didn't have the heart to compose a happy image anymore. So I told him it had been different.

    "Good different, or bad different?"

    "I ended up in the nurse's office."

    "Everything alright?"

    I started to answer him, but some guys walked in and started talking to him. I didn't care, I just packed my bag to leave. And I could have walked away, but I didn't.

    "So anyway, she thinks I might have had a panic attack."

    "Oh. Well, let me know if there's anything I can do."

"I'm alright. Thanks, though."

"Well, take it easy, Jess. Hope the rest of your day goes better."

"Yeah, me too."

And I made my way to band, thinking the worst of the day was over. I just knew I'd have it made in there. No, not me. The one thing I have never been able to understand in his class, and probably the easiest thing he teaches, is simple and duple time signatures. He calls on me, one of the seniors who the freshman thinks just has to know everything, and I give him the wrong answer. But before that, I was called out for having my mp3 player too loud, which I was sure nobody else could hear. I made an effort to turn it down low so that no one would hear.

Stupid things worry me. I dwell on stupid things. Everything I do is stupid, right down to the words I write.

Jessie

Friday, January 9, 2009
Dear Diary,

When I came home from school today, I found a package waiting for me on the table. Not a box package, but a heavy envelope. I laid Benjamin down to open it, and I really couldn't believe it. Okay, let me start over:

I had entered an essay contest a long time ago. A long, long, long time ago. As in, it's been almost two years. I remember going into the post office to send off my writing, and I had procrastinated, as I typically manage to do when I have a million things going on at once. I had assumed since it was postmarked before the deadline, it would still be allowed in the contest. Well, I never heard back from them after that.

Anyway, I open the envelope, and along with the essay

I've written and a few other things, there is a letter apologizing to me for not allowing the essay into submission in 2007, and congratulating me on taking third place in the contest for 2008. At first, I just put it back on the table and went on. Because first, I've noticed that if you win a contest, the only thing you've won is the opportunity to buy something. And second, I had forgotten that there were actual prizes to this contest.

    I find my essay later and read it to remember what I had written, and was going to put it all away for keepsake, since my computer crashed and lost the writing. And then as I was putting the papers away in my little box, I saw, "Congratulations on winning 3rd Place for the 2008 Contest Year." Right below that, there was a list of things I could use a $3,000 scholarship for. I can use it at any school in the country, for any enrollment program, and I can spend it on anything I feel I might need for school.

    But you want to know what's funny? I was telling myself this morning that there's no way I can go to college, and I'm stupid to think that I can. Just thought it was something to mention.

                                                       Jessie

Monday, January 12, 2009
Dear Diary,

    We have a lot of birds that fly around our house all year long, even in the winter. I always wondered how they made it through the cold, but they obviously got along alright.

    I looked out onto the little trees in front of our front porch, and the birds were picking the berries off the limbs. I guess that's how they survive each year; our trees.

If God will take care of even a bird, then... I must be scum.

Jessie

Tuesday, January 13, 2009
Dear Diary,

Today was actually a pretty okay day. I composed a new short piece, and there were only a small number of moments that sucked... The first moment occurred in English class, when we were choosing what personal narrative piece to add to our senior portfolio. I had the largest folder out of anyone, and all my pieces were garbage. So I begged my teacher to let me use a song, but she said it had to be a piece I wrote for a class. So what do I say? "I can write another one."

"It would have to be in tomorrow."

"I can do it."

Trying to force inspiration in times of desperation makes for a really bad piece. And I don't have anything to write, so now I've got that to worry about. What makes it even worse is that my grandmother has had Benjamin all night so I could get it done, and I still haven't been able to find an inspiration. At this point, I may just have to choose a bad piece that I already have and try to make it over. I had a really good literary piece I had written for Mr. Jones's class one year, but it wasn't in the folder, and it's not saved on the school computers. I wish I knew what had happened to it, because it really was a good piece. And that's saying something, considering I'm horrible with fiction, and rarely attempt it.

Durnham sat down and talked to me at lunch. She saw me writing my music and said she was impressed. "Does Jones know you compose?" I told her that I wasn't sure. But she wanted to know what I thought they could do to make the music department better and to draw more to it. I told her funding, funding, funding, competitions, and funding. I don't think it's that people don't want to join Band, but they just can't afford an instrument. And the best we have is a bass that looked like it came over with Noah on the ark, and a tuba that looks like it has seen MUCH better days. Competitions would be nice if we wanted our musical self-esteem shot in the face.

I ran into Tamson before seventh. I should have been happy, right? I was, until I just broke down and showed her how stupid I was. She asked me if I had gotten my application in for Murray. I lost it, saying that I'm a bad mother and that there's no way I can go to college now. I started to tell her to just forget I had said anything. But I was so stupid, I kept going. I guess I just saw her, and hit a point where I couldn't take it anymore. I've been about to crack for a while now, so I guess it's only a matter of time before someone breaks me. She told me that I was getting into college whether I liked it or not, so I guess we'll see who's right when the time comes...

After that, we had an infernal band rehearsal. The student conductor was getting frustrated because he was rushing, and the trumpets were dragging, so that made for a great time. Nobody was really taking him seriously, so no one was paying attention on when to come in, or anything. It really sucked. And when I talked to Brice tonight, a saxophonist whom I've been speaking with on facebook, he said that very few people showed up for the game. So you know what's going to happen in band tomorrow. Pep talk for the pep band.

On the plus side, I've really, really taken an interest in psychology lately. It's actually been taking up most of my free time. Not because Carson told us to do some major assignment, I've just been choosing to find articles and research and read them for entertainment. I learned that Ivan Pavlov was an awesome scientist, going so far as to define modern science even on his deathbed. He told one of his students to make observations in his final moments as he lay dying. He also wrote The Behaviorist Manifesto, and graduated from college at the ripe old age of 21, entering when he was only 16. You can also call an impulsive person Pavlov's dog, because of his experiments with conditioned and unconditioned responses.

John B. Watson probably need a little psychology himself, the jerk... But he did make a few significant discoveries. He was famous for the Little Albert experiments when he tortured this little kid to find out if fear could be taught. After he recorded his findings, he published several articles that told parents to think of the learning environment for a child as a scientific laboratory, that we are solely products of our surroundings.

Everyone kept telling me to take archaeology, that it was so much easier. I'm SO glad I didn't listen! If nothing else, most all of my other classes are full of stupid people and their antics, and Psychology doesn't house anyone like that. It's nice to get away from the ignorance for an hour a day.

Jessie

Thursday, January 15, 2009
Dear Diary,

I've gone through the biggest part my high school life already. I've seen people. Most of what I've seen is that which lies on two sides of a fine line; on one side, these people are bubbly, happy, bouncy, can't wait to get up in the morning. Then there's the other side, where those people are calm, cool and collected, more reserved to themselves and what the remainder of their lives is going to bring. Then there's a shadowy area with a few people, and these are the most fascinating...

These people are the ones that are on this earth who... Really would rather be just about anywhere else. Pluto, maybe?

In a grave? Hell would be alright, considering they've come to believe it through their miserable lives here. All the while, there's a God in heaven that's throwing new life on this earth all the time. And He knows who's going to love every moment they're alive, and who's going to wish they could hurry up and die when they don't have the nerve to do it themselves. Why not just create THOSE people? If God would stop creating such miserable people, we wouldn't have any gloom in this world. But instead, these people are just a burden to the other two groups of people until the day they die.

    I'm not sure what I'm trying to say. Just...why does God give people life who don't care about it at all, and especially when they can't even bring themselves, too. If you're going to create that sort of person, at least don't give them the will to feel better. Then, it just makes the whole thing a lot more sad...

Jessie

Saturday, January 17, 2009
Dear Diary,

    I've mentioned this before, but I've really fallen in love with my psychology class. I find the human mind to be a fascinating thing, particularly my own. Come on, who else is more complicated than me? Honestly.

    Anyway... I think the reason I like it so much is because it makes some parts of my life make sense. For instance, we talked Friday about how you can implant a memory into someone. We watched this happen on a short film where an adolescent had been lost in a shopping mall. He talked about running through the store, scared he'd never see his family again. Then he recalled a man in a flannel shirt finding him, and his mother running up to him. The psychologist conducting the experiment, whether having told him herself or enlisting help from the family to tell him, finally had to tell him that there was no man in a flannel shirt, and his mother wasn't there that day. He had been repeatedly told that there was, so he finally convinced himself of the false memory.

    This scenario has always applied to me; I would hear stories my grandmother had told me, and I convinced myself that I remembered them. But hearing this, it makes me wonder if everything I know is wrong. Isn't that scary? All of our memories may just be those that we've created, or other people have created for us.

    Well... Point being, maybe I shouldn't jump to too many conclusions on my mom just yet. I know she never earned the World's Greatest Mom mug, but she might not have been as bad as Mamaw made her out to be.

                                                    Jessie

Sunday, January 18, 2009
Dear Diary,

    I can't tell you how much better I feel after getting a whole six hours of sleep. And if six hours makes me feel better, that just goes to show you how little I'm sleeping these days. And it's not really that I can't sleep, I just don't have the desire to. Sure, in class on some occasions, I'll have to fight just to keep from crossing my eyes from exhaustion. But the minute I get home, I'm wide awake, and I have no desire to sleep. I'm going a mile a minute, writing this, rocking the baby, back to the drawing board, rock the baby, write another song, finish before the baby cries, change a diaper, write an entry. I feel like a meth addict. Not that I'd know what one of those felt like, but I can imagine it now.

    I'm either about to fall over asleep, or I'm after several

goals at once. I don't know what's changed. And the transition is so fast. Literally, it's as quick as a noise. If I were about to fall over right now on my computer, if I heard Benjamin crying, or I got a new idea for a song, I would snap into the equivalency of having been caught on fire. ...I've always been crazy, but I don't know what's gotten into me lately. I've never felt like this before.

    I wrote five songs last night. I couldn't believe it! I was up until four in the morning, and I finally got them all out. I was pretty tired after that, but then after listening to my composition again, I swore up and down that there was one sour note somewhere that was ruining the whole piece. The counter on the software said I played it 46 times, and I never found it. I didn't get into bed until about 5:30. But when I woke up at eight, I was wide awake. See what I mean? And I was ready to jump back on here and write some more.

    All I've been doing lately is writing. Before, that was just all I did at school, since I never did find the teacher particularly interesting. I've already filled up two notebooks since I've been back at school. I can't believe some of the things I've written, either. It seems like it's really, really good, or it's something you would expect out of a kindergartner's diary.

Jessie

<u>Monday, January 19, 2009</u>
Dear Diary,
    I don't see anything working out at this point. I wasn't going to be able to afford college before, much less now that I have a baby. It's not Benjamin's fault, and I'm not sure that it's not completely mine. Marrying the father isn't even an option, and I can't raise a baby with a high school diploma. So it's either marry the father, or find a way through college. So if I can't go the first

Where My Ink Comes From

route, and there's no way the second can work out, where does that leave us? Leave Benjamin? 'Cause I'll tell you the truth, I could care less what happens to me.

I'm still having my internal battle between nobility and stupidity. Nobody would see me as noble. Selfish maybe, or incredibly stupid. But noble? Brave? Anything but. And life has its way of hurting, particularly lately.

Yet again, one of those moments where I have a million things to say, and no words to use. How do I say something without really saying it? I don't know, short of maybe I'm just a lot crazier than I'm making myself out to be. I want to say some things, but I know I can't. Just like now, I'm painting circles all over my canvas. I haven't yet said anything of importance, or anything that's going to enlighten anyone, or somehow amuse their day. I think I'd rather be hated anyway than have to be around someone that doesn't care at all. Maybe that's how it is for Benjamin.

Don't misunderstand what I'm saying; I love my son to death, and I'd do anything I could for him. But the situation, everything with his father, and my not feeling like a mother, there's no way I can give him what he needs, much less what he wants. And I wish more than anything that I could tell him this, and he could understand. But right now, all he does is look at me, or go off to sleep. I held him one day and cried, telling him all of this. What I would have given in those moments to have him know what I was saying... I do love him, more than he could know.

But what am I supposed to do? All nine months, it was, "Be a mother or be like your own mother." That was ALL I would ever hear. Nobody asked me what I thought I should do, because they all decided it for me. And if I had things my way, my son would have grown up a lot happier. But no, ""Only a monster could give their child away!" No, a monster would leave her children before they could even crawl, call their father everything but white, and force joined-custody just so she could have the weekends to torture them. THAT would be a monster, and I am NOT my mother.

I never told anyone this before, but seeing as no one is going to read this anyway, and I might as well be honest with someone... Did you know that my mom drove my dad to suicide? Of course, he didn't go through with it; he's still here. Mom couldn't find him one day, and called my grandmother to say a gun was missing. Everyone went looking for him, and he had gone into the woods to kill himself, all because of my mother. He was going to leave us, but it would be horrible for me to leave my son, is that it?

As long as I'm telling stories here, here's another one: I have memories from very, very early in life, so early that I questioned them for a long time. In writing the story Daniel suggested, I was forced to analyze things more closely than I had in the past, and it's opened the door to a lot of details I had erased. There was a bathroom leading to my little brother's bedroom in the apartment Mom had at the time. I guess I was two, three at best. I snuck into the nursery where he was sleeping, for whatever reason, I don't remember why. But Mom decided to lock me in the bathroom. I thought maybe I had locked myself in, and maybe she didn't hear me. But looking back, it was a small apartment. She ignored me because she locked me in. I remember screaming as loud as I could, running back and forth to the two doors, begging her to let me out. For a long time after that, I couldn't lock a door, out of the fear that I wouldn't be able to open it again. I still won't lock a door unless I absolutely have to, because I'm afraid the lock is going to get stuck, and I'll panic if it does.

Here's another one: My mom was beating my little brother one night with a belt. I don't know what he did, I'm not sure where it was. I just remember she took him off into a bedroom, and used my Dad's belt to beat him. He was screaming of course, and when she finally came out, she shook the belt at me and my older brother and said, "You'd better shut up unless you want some, too!" I remember those words exactly. She was wearing denim shorts and a yellow t-shirt. She had her long, curly hair then. She was wearing tennis shoes. I'm not sure where my Dad was. My little brother doesn't belong to him, but I'd still like to think if that was happening, he'd step in and stop it. My dad doesn't care about the things I do, but he's not cruel.

There was another time when I was really messed up. I was a little bit older then, and I could remember bits and pieces of it. I was seven, and it was the summer before first grade. I was at my Mom's in Nashville. I remember the duplex with the little front porch that had the green swing. I would sit on it every day and watch a cocoon on a pine tree. I was hoping the butterfly would come out before I had to leave. There was a big backyard. I remember a fence, but not so much what was in it. Me and my little brother tried building a fort out of sticks that looked like bamboo. I'm not sure what it was. We finally gave up and just leaned them in a neat little row on the fence and curled up under them with a sleeping bag. Mom and my older brother snuck out and tried to scare us. Cody was scared, but I told him it was just Mom and Eric. Mom said to come in so we could go to bed.

I don't remember what happened after that. I only remember coming home and saying that I wasn't Jessie. I woke up one night and was staring at my face in the mirror. I remember saying exactly, "My face. It doesn't look the same." And I was scared, because I really looked different. I was taken to a doctor the next day, and he said that I had been drugged. He couldn't confirm anything, but suspected that I had been given too much LSD, and that I should see a child psychologist. It took a year to get me back up to par. Mom didn't make an appearance the whole time; I think she knew.

I have so many like these, some I don't think I'd ever be willing to tell anyone. These were the good times, compared to others. I could tell you about being locked in closets, having cigarettes put out on me, being thrown against walls, and going a whole weekend without being fed or changed, just to name a few. And the whole time, my dad can't do a thing to stop her. Writing the story brought all this up, I guess. I didn't mention some of these in that writing yet. And some I mentioned in that, I haven't here. There's so much, and I don't know if I can bring myself to acknowledge it all at once.

    Jason, one of my friends from Owensboro, was in the military. He's been home for a while, and I thought his tour was just over. Come to find out, he was discharged for Depression. I never would have known it; he always seems so happy. It makes me jealous of him, that he can feel the way he does and still be the way he is. Maybe he doesn't have the bad memories to accompany it, though. I wish I could be like him. So, besides feeling like the only purpose I have is to prove God makes mistakes, worrying about how to keep from being other people's burden, wondering which day is going to be a good day to jump, if I should jump, and having no one that really cares at all, I don't even have the chance anymore to change things. This is going to be my life until the day that I die. And I really, really don't want it to be...

                                                 Jessie

<u>Wednesday, January 21, 2009</u>
Dear Diary,
    You know what gets me is, people assume too much. Brice said it best: "I'm not as stable as people think I am."

    Actually, as much as I hate to, it might be time to have a long-overdue chat with Jones. I hate doing that, because I always know exactly what he's going to say, and I only leave feeling dumber than when I went in. Like, "Oh, of course, I should have

Where My Ink Comes From

known that." And I'm afraid that this topic of conversation, should I even get the truth out, is just going to make him say how stupid I am. And I am, I'd just rather it be said behind my back. If I can ever get out of third...

...Oh, that's another interesting subject matter for the day. Brace yourself for this one; I don't get to practice at home with the baby. And with auditions coming up, I REALLY need to. So my idea was to go during Jones's planning period, JUST on Fridays, so I could PRACTICE. I went one Friday, the day we had the fire drill, and that's been something like three weeks ago. And I've asked that teacher on three different says since that day if I could go to Jones's room. Each time, it was, "No, not today." So I was going to ask him again today, and he just said, "No, we're not going to do that." And the way he said it, I didn't say anything back, and just left him there. I wasn't sure what he meant by his tone. But when we get in the classroom, as he's shutting the door behind him, I hear, "If you were going in there to practice, it'd be different. But you're not going to waste time when we've got stuff to do in here."

So, here's the first reason I'm angry: His attitude in saying this was one you would expect to hear being used on someone who just got caught smoking in the bathroom. Besides not even being there long enough for him to know whether or not I was a trouble-maker, all I had done was asked him a simple question. Second reason, there's someone in that class that does get into a lot of trouble, wears all the black clothes, has a black mass of eyeliner, one of those. Because I'm not blowing this guy off, I'm actually talking to him, I'm automatically associated with that. So this teacher assumes that I'm a part of that crowd.

And let's throw this one out here, too: What on earth did he THINK I was doing in there? I wasn't going in there to look at the walls, or smoke in the practice room (someone did that my freshman year). I wasn't meeting with some foreign resistance group that was plotting to take over the school. What was he thinking? That I was just going in there to have a cup of coffee? Mull over the weather with Jones? Think about it! It should have occurred to him that a Bando, wanting to go to the band room, a senior, was going in there to do something besides waste time. My waste of time is sitting in a class and studying what I'm never going to use in life, and all because some higher authority decided we had to have it. Wasting my time means I'm not practicing my music when there's a VERY IMPORTANT audition coming up at Murray State University that will define my acceptance into the college, and ESPECIALLY when I'm not ready for it, regardless of what class it is. As far as I'm concerned, if it's the weekend, I'm not practicing, and my son isn't crying, there's something wrong.

So now that he knows I'm not going in there to pick my nose, I might actually get something done...

Anyway, I'm headed to bed. Sleep deprivation seems to be my enemy these days...

Jessie

Thursday, January 22, 2009
Dear Diary,

I feel like I'm trying to protect a Jew from the Nazis in the middle of Germany. I'm not sure what would happen if I made Benjamin's father known... Probably nothing, but I can't help but feel like I need to keep the truth to myself... Tamson suggested that I write a letter to Benjamin about his father. So I wrote one for him and put it in an envelope in the back of his baby book. I wrote "Don't open until after you're 16..." on the front. I figured by then, hopefully, he'd be mature enough to handle it. But I'm starting to wonder if he ever needs to know. But then to tell him, or anyone, why I'm not mentioning who the father's name is to tell who it is, so I can't even give a subtle hint. How would I tell

Where My Ink Comes From

him that it was for his own good he didn't find out and then explain why?

There's my internal battle again: Is what I'm doing noble, or is it just incredibly stupid? Am I trying to protect my son, or am I trying to protect me? I'd like to think there was a fine line between the two, but I'm starting to wonder. Maybe it all depends on who you ask. There might be some who actually understand it. And then, the others who are just positive that I'm crazy...

You know what? Today, I started thinking about way back to my childhood. Back before things got so hard, before the incident with my mom. I remember being happy. I had a little pink dress that I loved to wear. I would put it on and wear a plastic crown and pretend to be a princess. I remember wanting a shimmering blue gown, just like Cinderella. And I wanted to meet Prince Charming at the ball, leave with him, and live in the castle. Other times, I wanted to be as beautiful as Pocahontas. I had a tan dress that I would put on without shoes, and I would ask my grandmother braid my hair so I could go outside and play Pocahontas. I would wait for John Smith to take me on his ship out to sea. Oh, that was another one; I wanted to be a mermaid so badly. Anytime I would take a bath, I would curve my feet into fins and splash around in the water like I was Ariel. I wanted to do nothing but swim all day, and play with dolphins.

After what happened with my mom, I stopped wanting to wear fluffy dresses and waiting for a prince to find me. I didn't play, or laugh, or socialize. All I did was throw tantrums all the time until my childhood was gone. I have nothing left to offer anybody. I've never done anything for anyone worth mentioning twice. My writing is a ramble, I'm FAR from an inspiration... Why am I still here?

I don't know what it is about this place that's keeping me here... I don't understand...

Jessie

Where My Ink Comes From

Saturday, January 24, 2009
Dear Diary,

  Last night got pretty bad. I figured after I settled down a bit, I'd get in here and rant about it. But my brother had left the computer on, and I saw where Brice was online. And thank God...

  I started by telling him that I had just sent Mr. Jones a writing of mine, and I wished that I hadn't, because he was going to be finding out things about me that I didn't want him to. Assuming he reads it, anyway... And there's things about me that I'm not ready for people to know. When I sent it to Daniel, I remember kicking myself, wondering what I had just done. So while I'm telling Brice this, I start telling him what I didn't want people to know... And I felt bad about it. I don't talk to people about anything, because I don't think it's the place of anyone else to have to carry me around as a burden. And now, I feel like I owe him. Well, I felt like I did anyway, in two different ways. In the first way, he had shared a lot of things with me, and I felt the need to tell him some things because of how open he was with me. But now that I've told him, I think I told him too much, and I feel like I owe him for dragging him into everything. But I think I shared too much.

  I need to say this. No one is reading, no one would care if they were, and I know it happened, so I might as well admit it. When I got pregnant, I didn't want to be with the guy. *And it wasn't the fairytale first time I thought it would be.* ...That was true on so many levels. Who it was, how it happened... I don't want to say that I was raped. In truth, I shouldn't be able to say that I didn't want to, really. I didn't yell, even knowing that there were people nearby that could have stopped it. I don't think I fought him nearly as hard as I could have. To make it even worse, I gave up fighting him. I wanted it to be over, so I just quit. I knew the longer I fought, the longer...

...I can't. Forget it...

I can't say no. When Venson, my Spanish teacher, said she wanted to read it, I couldn't turn her down. So I told her I'd give it to her at the end of the day, and I spent my time looking over it, dreading what she would find out. After that, I was sure I was ready to let Jones read it, but I wasn't. I wasn't ready for Daniel to read it, but he's a writer, and I didn't mind it as much. Besides, I volunteered it for him and Jones. I wish I hadn't. People already see my past in who I am now. I don't want to taint their opinion of me anymore than I already have... I'm already called a whore among other colorful names, I don't want to make it worse.

See what I mean about my demons? I go around in circles. I can't even think straight, especially not these days. I've got so much on my mind, I can't sort it out. I've lost my focus lately. All I do is write, and short of what I've done at school, I haven't practiced. And music is all I've got going for me, if anything. If I can't do it or I don't have the will to, where does that leave me?

Brice tried to tell me how much I had going for me, and how much I had to live for. He talked about my son, and my writing and my music... He told me people loved me... I would've laughed if I hadn't been crying.

Jessie

Saturday, January 24, 2009
Dear Diary,
    This all seems unreal to me. I can't believe what

happened a year ago. I can't believe that I was ever pregnant, or that there's a baby sitting behind me. Worse, I can't even believe he's mine. I wish more than anything that none of this had ever happened. I love him, but he shouldn't have been born like this.

I don't know what I should do...

It's on my mind everyday. I had thought that I could just forget it, but I know I can't. I'm scared to be in the same room with other men, and I don't want people touching me, not even a hug. Mr. Carson wanted to talk to me about a play I'm writing yesterday, and I had to be in the room alone with him after the last girl left the class. I trust him, and my own logic says that he would never hurt me, but my own fears wouldn't leave me alone. I felt disgusting just being there, in the same situation all over again. I think it just reminded me...

No. I'm not doing this to myself...

                                                Jessie

Sunday, January 25, 2009
Dear Diary,

I did the same thing to Daniel last night that I did to Brice. I don't know why I do this to myself... Me? Jess, you should be worried about other people, not you.

We had been talking for a long time on facebook about how horrible it is to live. He asked me what was so wrong with me that I couldn't fix it. I told him everything. My talents are nothing short of mediocre, regardless of what other people think. I'd be fortunate to say my skills surpassed others in this county, and that doesn't say much where I'm from. And my skills don't do even that much. There are MUCH better writers and MUCH better musicians just in this town alone than I could ever dream of being. And if I can't compete on my own turf, how do I repeat with everyone out there?

    I still don't know how I was accepted into GSA. I guess it was mere luck. Actually, I'm not convinced that I wasn't just alternate for someone else who couldn't make it. They would have told me though, right? But who cares? I put more work into that than anybody else did, and for what? To find out I was pregnant three days after the audition. And what else? To find out that all my effort to make everyone proud of me had been wasted. My one chance to get into a place that might give my talents an ounce of hope of improving, and I screwed it up, like I do everything else...

    When my efforts are meaningless, what's the point in trying to achieve anything? My songs are mediocre, my music sounds like what a seventh-grader might pull off, my writing is nothing but rambling, and I don't have the talent to inspire anybody. I don't have the will to try anymore.

    "...I can't fix my life, Daniel." That's what I told him. Either way, I can't change what's already happened. Be a mother, or be like my own mother, right? 'Cause let's face it, the worst thing I could have done would have been to his benefit. My decision or what I feel is best for MY child should never be considered. After all, I'm too stupid, too young, too ignorant to ever make a decision by myself, and I shouldn't have the right. Better seen rather than heard, I guess... It tends to be my main goal lately...

    I'm not finished deleting garbage, either. I'm so sick of my mediocre talents... I hate using that word on myself. But if I don't want to use it, maybe I shouldn't be it. I'm deleting my music, and I'm going to keep only the ones I feel are worth keeping. I'm not even going to try to fix them, because I'm not a miracle worker, and God has better things to do than help me make one happen. Maybe I can start over again and build a whole other collection, one that the bad songs never get to see. No, I think that's what I'm going to do. I'm tossing out the bad songs, keeping the good, and if my writings aren't enough to surpass for mediocre, I'm not going to waste the space on my computer. I haven't taken myself seriously enough, but if I don't want to stay where I am now, I'm going to have to act like it and get busy.

Jessie

Monday, January 26, 2009
Dear Diary,

    I had to stay home from school today. I know there's going to be a lot of days like this, which makes me wonder why I'm even trying to graduate. I could drop out now and spare myself the trouble of living in events that are leading up to one big failure, because I know in the end, there's no justifying what I'm doing. I'm not sure which I would rather have: A career mom with next to no involvement with me, but gives me everything I need and want, or a mom making minimum wage that has everything to do with my life. I don't want my son to be materialistic, but I want him to be able to have all the things that other kids have, and not have to save up and plan months in advance when he wants something. But I would want him to have a mother, too.

    But he doesn't have much of one anyway, does he? I never know what he wants, or what his cries mean. This schedule that my dad and grandmother say he has, I don't know it. I don't even know if he really does have one. I don't get to make any decisions for him; THEY say when he goes to the doctor, THEY choose what he wears, THEY decide if he needs gas drops, Tylenol, when he needs it, how he gets it... They give him suckers! What do you think is going to happen when it comes time to feed him when, for two months, all he's known is sugar? He has no mother. He has a great-grandmother and a grandfather, and I'm just the babysitter. Babysitters don't get to make decisions for other people's children.

      If they're so unhappy with how little involvement I have with him, then when I go to feed him or change him, when I dress him, when I give him a toy, rock him, walk with him, play for him, maybe they should stop waltzing over there like they're his parents and take him, mumbling something stupid along the lines of, "You don't know what you're doing." You're right, I don't. So why don't you give me half a chance of learning? Oh, but I forgot... When I go to college, I don't get to take him with me. I have to leave him here, or I'm just like my mother, so it doesn't really matter that I don't know what I'm doing, does it? I'm just helping them out before I leave.

      Except I'm not going anyway. After all, I don't want to be a horrible monster like my own mother and try to make a better life for Benjamin. I'm stuck here. And nobody even cares that maybe what I want for him, maybe those standards are a little bit higher that the life I've lived. But I don't get a dog in that fight since, you know, he's not mine. I didn't give birth to him, or anything... If they insist on being the parents, why do they even need me? They're obviously doing a much better job that I could ever do, so why do they want me around? Why not just give up now? Why not just die?

                                                             Jessie

Tuesday, January 27, 2009
Dear Diary,

      The ice storm began about five hours ago. I laughed at the news because I just knew this thing was going to amount to nothing short of a white dust. Our news tends to exaggerate things. A lot. So I guess we'll see how this turns out. I about went crazy in last year's ice storm when the power went out and we didn't have any heat. Hopefully, this will stay within my original theory.

  Although in defense of the news, I just got done taking the dogs outside, and I have icicles in my hair. They weren't lying about that part. Oh, but the dogs were fun to watch. They weren't aware of the ice, and at my house, there's a ramp that my grandfather had to use before he died that we never turned into stairs. And they always make a mad dash for the yard, so they ran without thinking... To say I peed my pants laughing is an understatement, because both of them yelped out of terror. One ended up sliding between a tiny gap between the house and the ramp, and the other, my bright poodle, slid in under the car. They both sounded like someone was beating them to death. And I can't really explain how funny it was to watch them go back UP it, because it was something you had to see for yourself. I was going to film it and put it on facebook, but it's gotten too thick since then, and it's not as slippery anymore. It WAS just pure ice. Maybe it'll melt in a way that I can still film it later.

                Jessie

<u>Friday, February 6, 2009</u>
Dear Diary,
  The power is still out (I'm living off a generator and an icebox), Benjamin ate for the first time, and he laughed for the first time, too... Okay, you missed a lot as far as Benjamin is concerned, but otherwise, I've been bored as humanly possible.

  I was telling Brice yesterday that if all this had happened last year, it wouldn't have been so bad. I would have been annoyed, but when you have a baby in the mix, it makes it a lot scarier. The first night, I had to sit up and watch him out of fear that a tree was going to fall on the room we were sleeping in, and when the water quit working, I was worried about how we were going to get water for his bottles when a huge tree was blocking our only exit into civilization. I worried if he was cold, or scared, or upset, because I know he was picking up on my stress. And to say I almost lost it is... well, quite an understatement. About three days into it, all I could think about was how I couldn't protect him during a little bad weather, so there's no way I could ever be a good mother when it came to the basics.

      Although I did learn one thing through this horrible mess... Mothers tend to pray for the simple things. I prayed for his health, his warmth, his happiness, his satisfaction, and his peace. I prayed that he would have water for his bottles, and a warm blanket to sleep under. We weren't prepared for the storm, and we paid a price for it. But Benjamin is asleep on the couch under a heavy blanket, the house is (somewhat) warm with our 50 degree weather, and his stomach is full. What more could a mother ask for? And at least it goes to show you, I must have some idea of what I'm doing... maybe...

Jessie

Thursday, February 12, 2009
Dear Diary,
      The secretary at the front office called Carson today to ask why I didn't order a cap or gown. I don't remember now what I said, but I'm sure I looked stupid, because I stuttered. I knew why, but I just didn't feel like telling him in front of the whole class. In truth, I'm not going to parade down a gym floor to have a thousand eyes on me at once. I couldn't take the weight of their looks. That, and I don't have anyone to walk with. I'm a loser, remember? No one wants to walk with me.

All the seniors ordered theirs today... All but me... I don't know how I'm going to graduate, anyway. That's reason number three... I don't want to spend what could be potential diaper money when I may not even get to graduate at this rate. I think I keep going back out of hope that I will, but reality sets in every time I have a positive thought, as to why I'm not allowed to think in that mind frame.

I finished my paper for English today. I completely forgot to turn it in to her, but nonetheless, it's finished. I guess it works better this way, because I can get feedback before I turn it in. Brice, maybe. I'm not sure yet. I thought about sending it to Daniel, but I know he's really busy, especially lately. Maybe I can get a halfway decent paper to turn in, because the piece now is a rough, rough, rough, ROUGH draft. My ideas are scattered, and I hate the flow.

Speaking of which, I wrote three new songs today. One is in dire need of work, another is really good, and the last one is excellent. Too bad my level of excellence is run of the mill to everyone else's potential.

Jessie

Friday, February 13, 2009
Dear Diary,
I got to go to a game tonight. It was senior night, something I've looked forward to since freshman year. I got to play with my Band, and even got a free taco courtesy of Jones's mad dash to Taco Bell. So why am I so unhappy...?

I got in a fight with my dad before going. He had been gone all day, and my grandmother had to watch Benjamin. Jones had told me I needed to be there, so I had to go. Well, there was no way I was going to take the baby, I was stupid to even think

Where My Ink Comes From

about it (what they said). I couldn't miss, either. I wasn't going to go at first, but I didn't want to feel Jones's wrath when I couldn't make it. He might not have been mad if I could have told him ahead of time, but our phone is still out from the ice storm, so I couldn't even call. So I left, extremely upset. To make matters worse, my dad would rather have been at his buddy's house like he is EVERY Friday than stand there as the proud father of a senior on that one-time night. I try to remind myself that he didn't go to high school, so he doesn't understand the importance of a lot of that stuff, but it's enough to tick me off.

    The fun didn't end there... I was so excited to see how things were operating this year in Band, I forgot how things had always been. I was really sad when I left, but at the same time, I was overjoyed. I've come to hate that place almost as much as I once loved it, and to finally have it all be over, no more sitting by myself, beating myself up for every little mistake, or feeling like they're all just laughing at me behind my back, is a joy beyond words. And I don't ever have to go back to that again.

    I'm almost afraid to say this... But this year has been my easiest, by far. I don't mean academically, but personally. I have a son at home that I never thought I'd have... A teacher that says hi to me when he sees me (I know it's pathetic that that makes me happy, but Carson is awesome)... A rediscovered talent (courtesy of Daniel)... Someone who finally acts like he cares, something I've never had ('Brice-thoven,' as we call him)... But maybe the greatest part is my old niche for convincing myself that it'll all last. At least this time is different, and I'm not to naïve that I can't move on when the end comes. I can't lie and say I won't miss it. I know I always will. But there's a bigger part of me that's come to accept transition with only a dash of homesickness and regret. Besides, I've noticed that I don't miss anything, really. Things I once had, I miss what they once were.

    Daniel asked me earlier why I do music. No one has ever asked me before, short of myself. I never did get back with me on the answer, either. But I honestly don't know who I do it for. I know it's not for me, that's obvious. I think that if I didn't care what other people thought, I would quit. When I was asked this, all I could come up with was how ignorant I am when it comes to spoken word. I wouldn't get my thoughts out if it wasn't for songwriting, but that doesn't do me any good either, because nobody reads it, so no one knows what's on my mind. I have music that I think, if I was someone else reading it, I'd be disheartened. That's not to say I pity myself, but I just wish the day would come that I wouldn't have to hide myself so much. I don't really care about people knowing things about me, but it's more that I don't trust anyone with the information. I wrote four songs yesterday, and one of them was about the hardest song I've ever written. I'd love to share that song, because I KNOW it's exceptional work. Later, I'll tell myself I've lied about its true beauty, but right now, I think it's wonderful. However, it's all my truth, and more words than I'm use to sharing. I keep hoping for the day to come that I finally write that one-hit wonder, and it's nothing but the truth that begins a chain reaction in many lives. I can dream, right?

Jessie

Tuesday, February 17, 2009
Dear Diary,
      I sent Tamson an email. When I got desperate, I had Carson send her one too, thinking that maybe she didn't recognize my email. When she got there, she pulled me out of Spanish, and we went into the conference room. I was so confident going in there. I just knew I was safe. And then, she dropped the bomb. "By the way, you know what sort of things I have to report, right?" Well, that crushed me. I knew teachers were required to

do that, but then I had to race through everything I had wanted to say to make sure it was safe. I didn't say a fraction of what I wanted to. I wanted to tell her what happened, and why I'm afraid for Benjamin, but I couldn't. I couldn't tell her how his father is making life horrible for me, like I know he'll do to my son because he knows exactly what buttons to push. I couldn't even tell her what really happened Sunday, and why it scares me to death. What am I supposed to do now?

Sunday, Benjamin's father showed up here. Everyone, including Benjamin, had gone to see my aunt and to take my brother up there to stay for a while, and I chose to stay home alone. I heard a knock on the door around two o' clock and, for some reason, I didn't pull the blinds back to see who it was before I opened the door. Had I done, so, I would never have opened it. My heart stopped when I saw who was standing there.

"I want to talk," was all he said. Diary, I'm so stupid. I should've known better. I was hesitant, but I followed him out to the driveway. Why did I do that? As soon as we got there, he said, "Why didn't you call me when the kid was born?" with a tone that I knew couldn't mean anything good. Why on earth was I such an idiot? This was all something else I could've prevented.

"Why do you care now?" And he slapped me. I wasn't finished. I was so angry, and it was all coming out at once. "You don't even want anyone to know who you are! Why would you want to be called?" He was only asking the question to torment me. Diary, he hates me. He wants to hurt me, and I have no idea why. How could someone ever be so cruel? He punched me that time in the stomach, and I fell to the ground. He tried to kick me, but I turned so that he would only hit my back. If he broke my ribs, I knew I wouldn't be able to go to the hospital. The strength behind him felt like a sledge hammer. I just covered my face and waited, the thought crossing my mind that he might very well kill me.

He finally stopped, and I could hear him breathing. He

bent down next to me and said, "Keep your fucking mouth shut. Next time you open it, I'll see what I can put in it." I laid there until he got in his car and drove off. The tires were so loud, I almost wondered if he tried to run me over. I don't want to think how close they were, because I never saw them. I only heard them from behind my head.

    I picked myself up, went back into the house, and looked at myself in the mirror. I started running some bath water to soak in. I was so sore. My face was dirty, maybe from the dust of the gravel, and my tears were leaving palpable streaks. Seeing the mess I was in just upset me even more. Given his insanity, he was also smart; he knew I wouldn't talk, and I wouldn't show anyone any evidence of his visit that I could hide. He didn't hit my face. My cheek was red from his slap, but his punch was to my stomach. All my bruises would stay under my shirt, hidden from the world. Diary, he knows I didn't tell anyone what happened. He just did it to make sure that I wouldn't decide to. He doesn't have anything to worry about. The secret of his crime will die with him.

    I couldn't tell the truth to Tamson, or to anyone else. I tried to talk to Daniel about it, but I couldn't even tell him. I was too embarrassed, I guess. I told him and Tamson both that there was a confrontation with his father, and that I was worried he would try to cause problems. Trusting Daniel's intelligence in knowing that calling in bigger guns would hurt me MUCH worse than it would help, I told him only slightly more. I told him how I was worried about his father coming in the house when I wasn't there to protect my son. No one knows what happened or who he is, so he can't be protected when I'm not there.

    In working up the nerve to do this in the first place, I kept telling myself that I've carried the torch as far as I can, and I had done an excellent job protecting everyone, but I deserved a break. I told myself, pass it off to someone else. Let them step in and help you. You can only go so far. But it didn't happen that way. I did learn one thing, though; I learned I need to keep my mouth shut and smile. The bastard was right. Breaking is just going to get me and Benjamin in trouble, so I just have to get back up, go on, and hide my secrets the best I can.

...

I feel dumber than when I first started. I know I can't win. I can only protect Benjamin, and do the best I can with him. You should have heard him today. He came this morning to visit my dad, and when I told him I didn't want him to hold my son, he just said, "That's alright. I'll get him when you're at school." And to think what could happen... And it would be on my hands, because I let it happen. I don't think he would ever hurt him. Tamson said I only had four months left, but as crazy as he is, a lot can happen in a few months. It only takes a second to hurt someone. And regardless of whether or not I think he poses a danger, that's not a chance any parent needs to take, under any circumstances.

My God, Diary... what am I doing? Why on earth am I here at school and not home with my son?

Jessie

Friday, February 20, 2009
Dear Diary,

My audition into Murray State's Music Department was this morning. It didn't go too badly. I messed up on one spot, but they weren't looking at the music, and I made it sound like I was supposed to play it that way. The judges seemed like they liked me, so I hope it's a good reflection of whether or not I'll get it.

But can I even get a degree at all? Today may have just been a waste of my time.

Jessie

Monday, February 23, 2009
Dear Diary,
      I've been staying with Mary since Friday night. Whenever we get together, we mix our knowledge and see what crazy concoctions we can come up with. We started talking about me trying to get into college as a single mom, and how, when the time comes, I'm going to best get out of the house without being hated for leaving. My Dad's proposition has been to keep Benjamin during the week, the WHOLE week, while I go to school. Mary doesn't understand, and I can't say I do either, why they're willing to do that, but my Dad says he's "not putting his life on hold."
      Let me explain something to you... When I got pregnant, I NEVER asked them to help me. I was going to do whatever it took to go back to school and get a good job to support us both. Not that I would ever need Benjamin's father around, but I was determined to do everything in my power to make sure I had no regrets about being a single mother. I was going to get a job, put him in an accredited daycare or with a good babysitter, and I was going to make sure he had a good life. I was willing to go on WIC because I was going to try to get from point A to point B. After that, I was going to make sure I didn't need anybody's help. My family volunteered everything they're doing from the get-go. And I NEVER asked anyone to put their life on hold for me or Benjamin.
      The reason this all came up is the same reason I didn't get to go to the last home game that I would ever get to play at. I never once asked to go to any of the games, and I never complained about it. I may have written about missing it now and then, but I have a clean record in the complaining department. I

gave up Marching Band, GSA, the first semester of school, Pep Band, 4-H, Music Honor's Society, and my pre-college music course. I gave it all up so I could be home with my son, and I never complained about having to do it, because I wanted to be a good mom. I sorted my priorities long before he ever got here.

Here's another story; I've always said that my Dad is the greatest man I know, and I still mean that now. But when Mom left, even though he was working most of the time to try to support us, he slacked after the started getting government help. So when his buddies wanted to meet up and play music, or he wanted to stay gone for days at a time, he left us at home with my grandmother. She raised us, because my dad never did what single parents are supposed to do. I ended my life as I knew it, because Benjamin had to come first. Neither I nor my brother ever came first to my dad. If there was something he wanted to do, it didn't matter that we were home waiting for him.

I told Mary what my dad said the night of the homecoming game. My grandmother had had Benjamin all day, and I thought it would be nice to give her a break and take him to the game to show him off a little bit, and my dad could hear me play. He NEVER comes to hear me play, be it games, concerts, senior night, it doesn't matter. He had other things to do. The last game, I thought any parent would want to be there, but not my dad. He would prefer to go where he goes EVERY WEEK than hear me play for the last time. And after all that, it was, "I'm not putting my life on hold so you can go to a game. It's nothing but a hobby."

Let me explain something to you... The best way to tick me off is to call my music a hobby. Say I suck, call me mediocre, but don't ever call it a hobby. And second, I NEVER asked him to put his life on hold, I just asked him to come to the game. But I don't understand how he thinks I asked him to just by doing like every other student does for a school function, I'm sure. I don't care if I am a mom; I'm still a kid, so he says. So why can't I be a mom and still have some level of normaGCy in my life?

    But the other thing is, if he's not going to put his life on hold so I can go to a game, how does he expect to keep Benjamin for weeks at a time? Call me crazy, but I think he would REALLY have to, then. He's stupid if he thinks Mamaw can keep him all day, as bad as her health is. And my God, aren't I going to school so I can get out of that hell hole? No, I know exactly what it is. They expect me to stay there the rest of my life and live off food stamps and welfare. I got news for them: Benjamin is my family now, so the way I see it, he's going to come first, regardless of what it is. When it comes down to their feelings or my son's well-being... well, I think you know which one I'm going to pick. They can stroke out and have as many heart attacks as they want, but it's not going to change what has to happen. And if I expect to be the good mother I aspire to be, I know I can't worry about them

anymore.

    I don't have the luxury of putting my life on hold like my dad did. I can't dump Benjamin off on anyone else. And I guarantee you, when the time comes, I'm going to go to EVERYTHING at my son's school that he has going on. I don't care if he gets on a sports team and doesn't do anything but warm the bench, I'm going to sit in the stands and admire how well he's doing it. And I'm going to scream louder than any other parent there, because my son is awesome. Daniel said that I did the world a favor by bringing Benjamin into it, and I'm going to make sure his father regrets what he did.

Jessie

Tuesday, February 24, 2009
Dear Diary,
      I got an interesting letter in the mail today. I hope it's a good sign…

Jessica,

It was great seeing you last week! We will be sending out official acceptance letters very soon, but I can let you know that the woodwind faculty have recommended your acceptance! You will hear about scholarships not too long after that. I am really looking forward to working with you in the fall. I think you'll find that Murray State is a very warm and nurturing environment for you to grow musically and academically. If you have questions, let me know. I'm here to help now and for the next 4 or so years (and beyond, for that matter)

Sincerely,

Dr. Rea

      …Please God, if you're listening… let me get in now. I can't have my hopes get this high and then be knocked back down again...

                                                           Jessie

Tuesday, February 24, 2009
Dear Diary,
      Remember that email I was so happy to get from Dr. Rea

at Murray? Well, turns out that nobody cares. Well, of course people at school are a little interested, because they aren't so stupid that they don't know how important this is to me. When I told my grandmother last night, all I got was, "Uh-huh. You need to go to bed. We've got to get up early in the morning."

I was tempted to wake my dad up and tell him, but I was sure I'd get the same reaction. When I told him this morning, I got a nod. So I thought, maybe he didn't hear me, so I said it again. "I got an email from Dr. Rea. I'm pretty sure I got into Murray State."

Nod.

So, I don't understand. Tamson is proud for me, Laura, Brice, Jamie, Mandy, even Daniel is. But when it comes to the people that I want to be most proud of me, they don't even care. Maybe they don't understand that this is COLLEGE, and their daughter is going to be the FIRST to GO! The first to graduate high school, for that matter. Why can't they be happy for me? I'd even settle for them faking it, at this point. But what's the point in even trying to accomplish anything if nobody cares? What am I trying to achieve?

Jessie

Thursday, February 26, 2009
Dear Diary,

I thought I was only recommended for acceptance, not that I was already in. Apparently, everyone I've talked to says that I was accepted, that that's what that letter means. I just hope they're right. But being accepted into Murray is only half the deed. If my FAFSA doesn't go through, I don't get to go to college, and I'm stuck here.

I've finally been shown a way out, and I know I can do it. Once I get there, if nothing else, giving up means going home, and God knows I want anything, ANYTHING but that. Especially when, by that point, Benjamin will be old enough to imitate what he sees, and I don't know if I could handle him if that happened. I guess I'd have to, but then I'd always have a little piece of home with me. The best thing I can do for both us is to get as far away from here as possible. And I know once I do, I'll be a lot happier. And Benjamin will have the opportunities I never had.

    I wish I could make someone understand. But once again, my lips are sealed...

Jessie

<u>Friday, February 27, 2009</u>
Dear Diary,
    The day wasn't particularly bad, anyway. I did let something get to me in band before realizing she was wrong. A girl was brought up that had had a baby, and the girl who mentioned it was talking about how her life is over, and she didn't want a baby, because she didn't want to be tied down. She said that she sits with her legs crossed now, rather than laid out. I don't know if any of that was directed towards me or not, but regardless, the bottom line of that came off as only whores get pregnant. I wish I could remember exactly what was said, but I was too busy cowering over my desk, hoping no one would look at me. Jones was saying the other day how as much as I had already been through, college shouldn't be a problem for me. I wonder if he really meant that, or if nobody wants to say what everyone is thinking. I can't do it.

Jessie

Where My Ink Comes From

Tuesday, March 3, 2009
Dear Diary,

  Daniel got my revisions back for me today. I had sent him a couple of songs I wrote recently. I hope he didn't put anything off for me, but I was on cloud nine... ten... when I got them back. Maybe now, that song will be worth saying I wrote it. If I could die knowing I'd written just one good song, excellent song, I wouldn't mind going...

  I haven't been able to write for two days. I wrote a cheap love song because I was so frustrated over having no new ideas or inspiration. I think I allow some emotions to block my creativity. You'd think a wide range would work to my advantage, but no, not me. I had to be complicated. I'm limited in my words, and my feelings outside that limit is fenced off, forbidden, unorthodox... for me, anyway. If I'm not crying out to Jesus or recommending His services, I don't know what to do with myself. I get a little lost when I get out of my comfort zone. When I get here, it's like a newfound freedom that I don't know what to do with. Being happy makes me frustrated, because I can't do anything with it.

  I can't feel like this, because I'm meant to write music, and I can't go past the fence and write anything worth hearing. I have to stay in that place that allows me to create art. But it's such a miserable existence, I almost wonder if it's worth the price. If I have to stay somewhere that drives me to... do stupid things, for lack of a better way to put it, my music might be better left alone. So, do I just quit? Oh, I don't think I could and still live. My music is all that's saved me in the past. I'm almost indebted to it.

  My other source of creativity block? I came to a harsh realization a few nights ago. Are you ready for this? Nobody likes 'Jesus music,' as it's called. But can I write anything else? I may have to if I ever hope to make a name for myself, but I don't think I ever could. I never have, really. I might have written, at best, three country songs, but that's out of... well over fifty, and they were NOT pretty country songs. As I've mentioned before, I don't do love songs, I make fun of them.

    Now, I've written songs that weren't romantic, or promoting Jesus in the slightest. And I think those songs turned out pretty good. But I can't come up with that stuff on a dime. They just came on off-days. With contemporary, on the other hand, I can have two or three good ideas a day, have them written out and ready to type before I leave school.

    I have a chance of being heard, whichever I decide to do. My chances are still low though, and contemporary drops those odds to almost nothing. And if the odds are against me regardless of the genre, it might be best to try other things. I don't know though, I don't think I'd ever be happy writing anything else.

Jessie

<u>Friday, March 6, 2009</u>
Dear Diary,

    Sometimes, I wonder how I write what I write and barely step foot inside a church. I barely think God exists in some moments. I know He must, but it's difficult to imagine when I reach a certain pitch. If He really is a myth, I don't want to know about it. It would just confirm that nagging fear in the back of my mind, that in trying to earn my salvation through the inspiration of others, I'm wasting my voice.

    I've become convinced that the measure of my life is defined through good deeds and debts repaid. My music is all I have left to offer anyone. If it's mediocre, I just have to write that many more to make up for lost talent. If my debts will be repaid by my meek voice, it may be the only way I have to pay it. But then, I feel a little guilty. The way I pay for my sin is through something I enjoy very much. I can't keep myself from feeling euphoric when I write a new piece I can be proud of. I shouldn't have the right, but what else am I supposed to do? I don't know how to do anything else, and I've accumulated quite a debt to society. I couldn't write enough music to pay it all back.

    I know the people I've hurt specifically. But I never understood why I felt the need to pay everyone else. Nothing short of believing that everyone who didn't have a choice to be in the presence of something so foul, I must give something in return for everyone's trouble. I'll not forgive myself until I believe I deserve it. I don't have the courage to take my own life, but I'm not sure anything I can ever do or accomplish will make up for my being so cowardly.

    I don't know what to do exactly. Maybe I'm just hoping for something better to come along in my life. I'll never admit the truth about the things that have happened in this house, anyway. Some things took place that I'm taking to my grave. Given the pain in my life has made for some wonderful sparks of creativity, I can't say it was ever worth the trouble. I'd rather be happy and lose all of my 'talent' than live the rest of my life with these memories. They disregard the entire point of living. How will I ever be happy?

                                                                      Jessie

Tuesday, March 10, 2009
Dear Diary,
    Nothing especially interesting happened today. Juniors had to do their ACT test today, so Jones's class had to go to another classroom. I got my picture taken for the yearbook in second (because I refused to allow Gene Boaz to take a senior picture of me pregnant), and filled out the sheet for the *Seniors* section of the yearbook. I got a rough review on my Spanish paper (there was a hint of an allegation of plagiarism). Who would think me capable of intelligent writing, anyway?

Murray received my application already. Now, the strange part is, I didn't send it. I got a letter in the mail today from MSU, telling me that they still needed my transcripts and the application's fee. The reason I hadn't sent it in the first place was because I didn't have enough money to pay for the fee and the housing deposit, too. Thus, I have to call my mother, and fast. I've tried all night, and I've yet to have her pick up the phone. Let me pretend for a moment that I'm surprised. Oh well... I'm still caught up in how they have an application for me when I never filled one out. Now, I did fill the application out on the website, but it was never sent. I was planning on sending a money order later when I finally had the money to, but that didn't happen. It was either have a credit card, or nothing at all. Guess which one I had... So I'm back to square one.

    I even bought one of those Visa cards everyone has been swearing by lately. I thought maybe I could use that to pay for the application online. Well, I have to have a bank account for it to work, and I don't. The card has to be registered first, and I had to open the package the card came in to get the serial number before I could be told it wouldn't work, and also that once opened, the card can't be returned. So, I paid $100 for a shining piece of useless plastic. Besides not getting to pay the fee, Benjamin is almost out of diapers, too.

Jessie

Thursday, March 12, 2009
Dear Diary,
    If someone had accused me of plagiarism that barely knew my name, who I'd met a few times, if at all, who read something I wrote that exceeded expectations, I would take it as a compliment. I would be overjoyed that I would be considered a

better writer than I should be at my age. Please accuse me of plagiarism and make my day, because I need to smile more.

The story behind this much-desired compliment actually began yesterday. Without actually coming out and saying it, in front of everyone, a teacher told me that I needed to give her my sources, because in her words, my paper sounded 'textbook-ish.' She said, "If they can Google your paper in college, they WILL throw you out." And then added a look that could easily have set someone ablaze . I always type up a cites page, and I'm not sure why I forgot to this time. I was annoyed, but I brushed it off. I just thought that maybe I was paranoid.

I got on a computer in second period and typed up my page of sources to give her. I printed it, gave it to her, and she said, "Sorry, I wasn't very clear. I need you to print off all of your sources." So she thinks I exaggerated to the point of needing to see word for word what I did? This isn't even a teacher that I don't know too well, or one that's high-strung enough to question everyone. This woman has known me all this time, knows that I write like crazy all the time, but God forbid I write something intelligent. Oh, I gave her the research. I printed off over 100 pages to keep her busy for a while. I didn't print off anything I didn't use, but maybe she'll realize that.

Today has been awful all around, though. I was late for school this morning, and my Dad didn't come to pick me up until 4:00. He was an hour late because he "looked at the clock wrong." You mean the ones I set myself? I'm not stupid; I know where he was (hint: he's in love). I made an idiot out of myself in third... don't ask... realized my letter wasn't finished for English class, made Carson think I was stupid when I tried to show him something I'd found on the internet... all the things in my head, I guess... Didn't make the day any easier, though.

I did get into a fight with my dad on the way home. He still wants me to drive to and from Murray everyday, like students don't have to live on campus, or anything. I dozed off a little while later at home, and when I woke up, I heard them talking while they thought I was still asleep; My grandmother said that I was going to leave him like my mom left me, because when I took him off to Murray, social services would take him away for my being an unfit mother. I told my Dad that if they didn't let me go when the day came, they had better be ready to fork over some money, because I won't live off of minimum wage and give Benjamin everything he really needs.

    I can tell you now that that will never, never happen. Because I refuse to rely on them anymore after May.

Jessie

Friday, March 13, 2009
Dear Diary,

    I am not a hard person to please. I take situations dealt to me in stride, and I put them away for later inspiration. I've seen places that are very dark, and I've come out with only a few scratches, so to speak. But you know, I'm blessed to have dysfunction in my life. Writers must have experience with some levels of trauma, or they can never reach into themselves for an emotion to portray. Of course, I've never been one to handle my own mind and emotions well, but I hide them easily. It's a beautiful gift to own. If I ever spoke out in an attempt to comfort myself, I'd lose my abilities.

    I'm not sure what's gotten into me the last few days. Well, I do, but it's nothing I haven't handled in the past. I've become quite used to having mediocrity expected of me, from school and at home. Actually, to have anything expected of me at home would be a blessing. I've become accustomed to being looked down on and being thought of as less of a human being as other people. Certain events took place in my life that finally led me to believe that something wasn't right about home. Had it not been for this realization, I might have turned out like my brother.

There have been various things play out in my life that led to situations and emotions I could never see an end to. In was in those moments that I turned to security, the only sanctuary I knew, and I made myself out to be the strongest person I knew of. My creativity has always allowed for a door to be built when there wasn't one in place. I've always found that I am at my best when I've hit bottom. At the very least in my comforts, my Bible made for a great pain reliever until I had rested long enough to get back on the front lines. What am I trying to say, then? I'm more angry than I am anything else, knowing everything currently wrong at this exact moment was all preventable.

I could've handled those accusations easily about a week ago. Any other time, only the normal things are happening that I've come to expect, and don't much bother me anymore. They do, but I can typically hide them pretty well (I think). I went to school still carrying the frustration of having heard what I did last night, and being thought of as a liar by a teacher that should have known better. No good was going to come out of today.

This morning, I stood in the attendance office for ten minutes waiting for the secretary to finish up her conversation. I don't know if it was important or not; I really don't care. But I finally left, because I was late anyway, and just went to class. I got to unwind in Jones's room during third while I practiced some of my compositions.

Typically, because I know I'll be asked to say it in Spanish, if I have something to do before 5th starts, I don't ask, I just go do it. But I had to go past the classroom, so I decided that the respectful thing to do would be to stop off and tell the teacher where I was going to be.

I didn't have a planner with our hall passes in it (I never got one on homebound), I can't speak Spanish, and she refused to help me until someone else had to go somewhere. Then she got angry with us both, and said, "I'm not helping you anymore. Today is it." So I left and couldn't even get in the office. I finally had the secretary leave him a note that I needed to see him about my grades.

During this horrendous hour of Spanish, I was called out for plagiarism. Our reports were brought up, and I said something about giving her the research, that I didn't have anything else to do. She was talking about another assignment, as another student pointed out, that I wasn't there to do. After giving me a look that could have set ice ablaze, I got this: "Don't plagiarize. Put it in your own words." And then tried to come over there talk to me about my topic as if nothing out of the ordinary had happened, like I wasn't turning red and hoping the earth would open up and swallow me.

I left there, and for the second time that day, felt myself breaking. I knew it was coming, and I was dreading it. I always have a massive headache for hours afterwards. I got out of it the first time. I was on my way to Psychology, when the guidance counselor stops me. I didn't even ask him about my grades; I was too busy with, "I want out of Spanish." After telling me I'd lose a credit, I told him I'd make it up at Murray. But some way I worded that, he said he couldn't do that, that it wasn't something he could write on my transcripts. I think he thought I asked him to lie for me, and I would never do that. So on my way to Psychology, thank God for Carson, he said hi to me from behind, and I stopped. I was almost begging him to let me go to the library. I had already started crying, and he was obviously concerned. "What happened? Did somebody do something? Are you okay?" I told him I'd talk to him after class, but I needed to go right then.

As I'm walking towards the library, I see two classes in there. So I'm going with plan B; the bathroom. I go to the farthest stall, and I lose it. I haven't cried like that in a LONG time. I tend to cry a lot of a mother's tears, but nothing like a fit. Knowing I'm not where I told Carson I would be, I'm trying to rush and put myself back together. I didn't want to stay in there long, knowing he was nice enough to let me go. I cried just as much as I needed to function, and I washed my face and left.

On the way back and in the classroom, I didn't look anybody in the eye. I knew what I looked like, and I didn't want to make it obvious. I was prepared to tell everyone, should they have noticed, that I had a sneezing fit. Providentially, no one noticed, so no one asked. After class, I sort of ditched Carson, because I wasn't fully prepared to bring on the waterworks again. I took Band in stride and went back to him, knowing perfectly well I owed him an explanation as to why I chiefly ran out of his class. So I told him the whole hideous story of the week, and I didn't even want to mention everything else on top of it. I gave him censored and condensed information, and for ONCE, a teacher acted like he cared.

I told Carson, Daniel, and Brice that I'd see them Monday. But the way this week has been, being in the same state that has caused me to do really stupid things, I don't think I can handle another day as bad as today. Especially when they've just been getting worse and worse since Saturday. Of course, I was home then, so something is just going to happen here. And at least at school, I'm better at hiding things. I don't know, I really don't need to miss. I've too much to do.

I also got an email from Jeremy, an old friend from post-baby. You don't need to know what he said. But it was over my not being at the computer while he was sending me messages that I wasn't aware he was sending. I finally got around to them after the baby had settled down, and he was already off. A couple of hours later, I got a message him. So I thought my trouble was over when school let out, but God forbid I see a break anytime soon. It was really nasty, to say the least. And I was so angry at everything and everyone else, he got in a line of fire. I wanted to break him. I sent him the nastiest, meanest, cruelest message my small mind could produce. I was in tears writing it, and felt horrible afterwards, because I've never done that before. I made fun of the drama queens that did. All I can say is, I owe him an APOLOGY. And I mean one of those ask-me-for-a-puppy apologies. Maybe I won't be so angry at him tomorrow, but I'm sure he won't be so forgiving. Of course, given I feel bad about it, ask me if I care. Go ahead.

  I talked to Daniel about my Spanish paper on facebook. It did seem to be the straw that broke the camel's back, or at least began the sequence. He told me not to worry about it, just as Coleman did. It's hard not to when on top of everyone whispering behind my back that I'm a whore that must've had sex fifty times ('cause you know, you can't get pregnant with one take), I'm now a liar and a cheater. Thank you, Green Central, and all of its inhabitants, for thinking me incapable and ignorant. Now I know what's expected of me.

  I have to wonder if my Spanish teacher judged based on other things I've written, and maybe she thinks that my paper was above and beyond what I could ever accomplish. I had come to tell myself lately that I am a good writer, with plenty of talent to share, but when something like this happens, I have to doubt myself.

  What was it Sue Grafton said...? "Cry, pick yourself up, dust yourself off, and get back to the task at hand," or something like that. I cried, I picked myself up, I dusted myself off, and now I'm ready to get back to my notebook. The joke is on everyone else, anyway; They hurt me, I write a song about it. That song is bought, and it turns into money. So for every time they beat me down, they pay a piece of my salary. Swallow that apple...

Jessie

Saturday, March 14, 2009
Dear Diary,
    My brother came home today... What really ticks me off is that when he goes away for a while, I'm supposed to enjoy it beyond what might be considered normal. The day he left was the same day my week turned horrible, so I have to wait for my next vacation to actually get one. I almost laughed out loud when I thought that I felt like that couple did on *Open Water*, when they went on vacation to get away from work, and then ended up being left in the water with an assemblage of sharks.

    Let's just add this to today's pot, too; I'm not trying to make a career for myself in music, but rather in the education of the idea. I don't expect to ever make a name for myself in songwriting; I'll never stop trying, but I'm also not oblivious to the odds of that ever happening. "You need to go on and be a nurse where you can have money and a good living, and leave the baby here, 'cause you can't take him off like that." Well, I'm sorry, but the only reason my dad wants me to make a lot of money is so that I can keep my brother up. And besides that, what's the good of having all that money if I never get to use it? If I ever had that much money, I'd buy a house as far away from here as I could be, and the only one I'm going to support and keep up is my son. Sorry to burst people's bubble of expectations.
                                                 Jessie

Sunday, March 15, 2009
Dear Diary,
    This time last year, I was getting ready to go to GSA. This time last year, I was missing school for those ever-elusive frustrations on 32-note runs, and indifferent to a bittersweet

promotion to senior. Later, it was this time last year that I went to my GSA audition, almost gave up, did give up, Jones got his three-day vacation, and I found out how tough I am as a musician. This time last year, I found out I was pregnant, refused to believe until the seventh, SEVENTH, month of pregnancy, and I realized that things had changed for good. This time last year, I came to the harsh realization that if nobody wanted anything to do with me before, they really didn't then, that I was going to be alone for the rest of my life.

I've come to realize that last year sucked, too...

It was the easiest I was going to have things be for a long time, though. I realize that now. Through the complications birth has brought (mine, not my son's), I've learned what to expect and what is, sequentially, expected of me. I've come to know what's important in life; my son, my music, my drive, and my scars. Each serves me one way or another. Each one, in its own way, has come to be my inspiration, or it has come to be my motivation. Sometimes both.

I know now that, had Benjamin never showed up, I'd still be lost. My family would still find a reason for me not to go to Murray. I'd still be calling Mary in tears, wondering how I was going to get out of this place that I hate so much, and I'd still be having meltdowns that would lead me to ditching out on Psychology class to go have a moment somewhere. I would still be having fights with people and I would still have been pushed to the point of sending a really cruel email to someone who probably didn't deserve something THAT harsh. And I would still be sitting out on my porch some nights, playing guitar and wondering how easy I could just give up and let all of the decisions be made for me. The only difference Benjamin has made is that he is the reason everyone is so angry with me for trying to make my own life and my son's life work. They would have found another reason, otherwise.

Here's my justification for not caring about them

anymore: I have someone else to worry about. College was a big 'if' for me before he ever showed up, but now that he's here, I am going to fight until I can't to make sure he doesn't have to grow up and see the things I've grown up seeing. And you can call this one selfish if you want to, I don't really care. But I would like to think that I had a lot more time left on this earth than either my dad or my grandmother. I may be egotistical, but I'm not going to sacrifice my being happy so that they can be.

  I had another weird dream that brought all of this up; it's the second time, too. I dreamed that GC was a tall, glass building, with several stories, and it was in the pit of a huge city with masses of lights. The first time, it was the actual school, so I don't know what the difference was. Regardless, I was in the teachers lounge with a couple of teachers, but I don't remember who they were. I think Venson was one, and maybe Carson or Jones. Maybe there was more than two. ...Anyway... things went dark, and a siren was going off. The alarms had lights on them that caused a red light to fill the place, and then fade out again. We thought it was just a drill, so we stayed put. Then another teacher came in and motioned for us to leave, that it wasn't a drill. We get out, and we realize that while the majority of students are out, several are still inside. The alarm didn't reach all of the floors. The bomb went off before the squad ever got there. We watched it fall, and people were screaming. Me and another student were together when we got out, and he was crying with his parents. I was there by myself, so I just started screaming. In the next scene, I'm walking through the students that managed to get out. We were all standing in the dark outside, and I remember a police officer was calling off all of the names in each class. The ones that didn't answer were obviously the ones that hadn't gotten out in time.

  In telling my paranormal-obsessed grandmother, I tried to remind her that a dream in itself doesn't mean anything much. The three teachers were the ones involved with this horrible week, and Jones asked me to go to the lounge Wednesday to grab a paper he had printed off. I was remembering earlier the time we had a fire drill at school, and I was in Jones's room alone, so I got locked out when I went outside. The student I was with that was crying with his parents, I sat next to him in the library and we talked for a few minutes. I was also thinking about that Lifetime movie where the woman has a stroke, and her daughter is in the shootings at Columbine a few years later. They were running the actual news footage in the movie, and they were saying that students whose name was running across the screen was accounted for, and anyone else hadn't been identified yet. And as for the school crashing down, I'm convinced that something is going to happen that is going to ruin any chance I may have at Murray. I just hate having dreams that I dwell on the entire day.

...I think I'm going to take the advice I've given everyone else. "All you have to do is lose your mind ONE TIME... And you won't have anymore problems with people." I think if I ever screamed loud enough to let them know that I was going to Murray to make a life for Benjamin and I meant it, they might let me be. I know if I keep sitting there like a princess and saying, "Oh, no, I disagree," I'll end up listening to them. "Well, if it will make you happy, I'll stay here. I wouldn't want to disappoint you."

Let me end this note with two words: Screw, conformity...

Jessie

Monday, March 16, 2009
Dear Diary,
...Everyone else might as well be sick, too. I had to miss school when Benjamin ended up with a 101° fever at five in the

morning. I couldn't find his thermometer, and everyone was angry at me for losing it. They wouldn't let me give him any Tylenol, either "It made him sick last time, he doesn't need any," was all I got out of my dad as far as an explanation goes as to why I couldn't give him any medicine to bring his fever down. The first time I gave him some, it didn't even have time to hit his stomach, and he had been throwing up, anyway. My timing was just really bad, and I knew that. I've never heard of an allergy to Tylenol. We had no way of knowing what his temperature was, and it could have been well over 102° and we never would have known it. Never having dealt with a sick baby before, I wanted to take him to the emergency room.

He finally got to the doctor's office at 11:15 this morning. Poor kid hardly cried, short of a whimper here and there. I can't believe how good of a child I have. The doctor says that he thinks it's the flu, that the season began later this year than usual. He ordered a flu test and a strep test. I thought I had held myself up well for this to be his first real illness until the nurse swabbed his nose and throat. While I was holding him, he was squirming so much, my Dad had to hold his head, and that's when my heart broke. He started screaming, and I wondered if he was thinking that I was hurting him, or letting someone else hurt him. I sank.

We waited another ten minutes on his test results to show which one he had. I was hoping the doctor was right about him having the flu, but he doesn't have either one. Now, with a rattle in his chest, I'm going to worry until we have to take him back Wednesday that he has something much worse than the flu. A lot of babies around here have turned up with pneumonia. That's all he needs; a preemie with pneumonia. He's certainly had all the luck so far...

We went to Wal*Mart afterwards, and I bought him the best toy I could find. Each time I found one that I thought he would like, I held it up to him. Most of the time, he just looked at it. I got a lot of dirty looks as I was talking to him, like mothers are forbidden to talk to their children in public. I finally found one of those Fur Real Friends animals, and I asked him what he thought. It was the first toy to get a reaction out of him. He grabbed at it and fingered the soft fur. I said, "You know this is supposed to be for a smelly girl, don't you?" He just smiled, and it was the first smile I'd seen out of him all day. Needless to say, that thing made its way into our cart really fast. Well, by 'into our cart,' it stayed with him most of the time.

  I realized in shopping for that toy that I got cheated as a kid. All the cool toys didn't come out until I was too old to play with them. I've had more fun with the dog than Benjamin has, so far.

  My brother has been home for three days now. While he was gone, Benjamin slept so much better. I'm sure it's because of the quiet that he takes longer naps. And it could just be me, but he seems less fussy when my brother isn't here. Besides the quiet his absence instills in this place, there's peace. There's no fighting, no harsh words, no yelling. Nothing is happening. Benjamin picks up on my stress, I think. Maybe that's why he's not as happy. I actually don't find myself enjoying my brother's vacations as much as I should, because I always spend too much time dreading the day he comes back. He can never just stay gone.

Jessie

Tuesday, March 17, 2009
Dear Diary,
  I found the most wonderful quote yesterday, and I fell in love with it immediately. It said, "Sadness doesn't do anyone any good. Only when you get mad can you bring about a change."

And I'm very angry... I don't get angry often...

  I could easily take harsh words being thrown at me. I have since 4th grade, after all. And I've always just let things happen, because I knew I deserved it. But there's also a point in which someone has paid back their debt, and then their torment is no longer justified. As I've mentioned before, I'm only a product of horrible circumstance, terrible circumstance, but I've almost defied all of that. I say "almost," because I haven't made it to graduation yet. There are certain people to be stood up to before that happens, and I'm only hoping that by then, I have the courage to do so. My point is, I've served my sentence. And even if I was a worse monster than what I claim to be, there are things that nobody deserves. At least, I think so. But maybe that's the part of me that's tired of being a criminal, too.

  Something else I've mentioned before is... I don't care what you say about me. I really don't. You can call me the most vulgar names, use the harshest insults, say the most ruthless things you can say about me, and I really won't care. I only start caring when they're said to my face. If there's a rumor going around about me, don't tell me. If someone is threatening to beat the crap out of me, I don't even want a warning. Now, I'll take anything thrown at me into stride. I won't draw any lines... until you pull my son into it.

  Despite what anybody says, I have NOT told anyone who Benjamin's father is. And I do mean ANYONE, right down to my little leather journal. NO ONE. And when I do, I won't be telling someone quite as ignorant as Jeremy. Brice knows a hint of what happened, and Daniel does, too. But Jeremy doesn't, nor anyone else, know who my son's father is. But even if he did, he had NO right to pull him into this. As angry as I am at him, if he had kids, I would never have done what he did, no matter what he did to me to begin with. Even Benjamin's father, and I can't imagine anyone I hate more, if he had other kids, I wouldn't touch them. (Although let's be honest; odds are, he HAS other children.

He just may not be aware...)

Daniel has brought out in me humility, pride, and honor, three things that I'd forgotten I had through the midst of everything that's happened. Only in this last year have I stopped becoming the very thing that I hate, and there could be no more weGCome change than this one. A year ago, I would have taken everything happening now to heart, and I would've ended up in the bathroom playing slice-and-dice. I'm not going to lie and say that the thought didn't cross my mind, but the only thing, I realized, that was going to hurt me more than his words was knowing what his words led me to do. And I wasn't in a state to feel worse.

When I got home, he tried calling me. Not Benjamin's father; Jeremy. One thing I recall saying to him in that ever-so-harsh email was, "I don't mess with ignorance." He doesn't seem to understand this, either. He called sounding calm, cool, and collected. Hearing his voice, I wasn't able to SPELL calm, cool, and collected... I just didn't let him know. The SHORT conversation was, "Jessie?"

"Yes?"

"Do you know who this is?"

"Yes." *click*

What else gets me is that the jerk had the audacity to call me with a blocked number.

Let me explain something; I've discovered in my 18 years here that there is a fine line between men and gentlemen. Men are morons, and think only with an organ a little south of the brain. For every 10,000 men, there is one gentleman. I've only had the pleasure of meeting two true gentlemen, one of which I discovered later wasn't so much of a gentleman. There are those in between, that I wouldn't consider to be a gentleman, but that's not a jerk, either. I haven't decided yet what to call this special breed, but I'll think of something. I'm going to give you three guesses where I rate the calm, cool, and collected genius mentioned above. I've only fallen in love once, and that's a place that I'm never going back to, only because I know the odds of ever finding another one.

So, I have to face everyone tomorrow, and I have to succumb to their harsh words and stares. And I'm going to take it, knowing that Murray is in sight, and that one day, Benjamin is going to beat their kids up. Here's to hoping that none of this crushes me in the meantime...

Jessie

Wednesday, March 18, 2009
Dear Diary,

I was hoping that nobody important was nearby to see it what I did today. I was so desperate to get out of there, I didn't stop to take note of who saw me. I don't know though, that kid deserved SOMETHING, even if I did take it too far. Still, there are some things you don't say. Ever. I don't even know who this kid was. He was tall, skinny, had curly blonde hair, very bold, blue eyes, and he was wearing a red jacket. He was one of the guys that dressed up as a cheerleader for a pep rally a month or so ago. He walked up to me and said, "Hey, who am I?" And he then proceeded to contort his arms and face up like a retarded person, and tried to run me over.

I knew what he was saying was in reference to what Jeremy had been telling everyone. Let's go ahead and say this one again; I really meant what I said when I said that I don't care what anyone does to me. But do NOT bring Benjamin into anything, and he did that today. Besides annoying me, he called my son a retard based on the rumor Jeremy spread. Without thinking, I shove him as hard as I can, and yell, "Would you go get fucked?!" I was distraught over the incident having happened, but when I finally got a chance to tell Brice about it, it sounded so stupid, I had to laugh.

If it had been the other way around, I would have been called a moron, an idiot, fill in the blank, for having done something like that. But he was popular, and I'm a freak. So naturally, everyone agrees with him. I made a beeline for the exit out of that circle, so I'm not sure how people reacted to it. Although I'm sure I'm blowing it up in my mind. People surely saw what he was doing, and if they had a heart at all, they sympathized. I wish I knew who he was, though. Even if they didn't, I'm sure the, "Did you see that?" conversation didn't make it to the classroom for any witness.

I don't lose my temper often. It takes a LOT for me to blow up in public. Now that I think about it, that's probably the first time that's ever happened. I keep thinking that there was one other time, but I can't recall what that was, if there ever was another occasion.

Shelby's mom (Shelby is a classmate in my 3rd period) came and talked to our class (she was awesome)... I haven't told Jones that my Flute is broken yet... My tendonitis is coming back really, really bad. I can't hold on to anything, my flute included. So as I'm practicing, this horrible pain shoots from the bend of my wrist all the way up to my forearm, and I drop the flute. Where I was at the time, it was just perfect to have the rod graze the end table, and now that part is coming completely off. I really didn't want to ask Jones to fix it, as busy as he's seemed lately, and it needed new keypads, anyway. So it's at Cole's now, and I really need it back, since we've performances coming up soon.

...Carson gave me a slightly-less-than-deserved compliment today, as well. I had to get my paper from him, so I walked down to his class with him to get it (he was in the library). When we got there, he was telling me how good my paper was, and how he was going to give me extra credit for it because I was a "model student, well-behaved, and never complaining." I was NOT worthy of that one. I tried desperately to argue, to the point that I almost wanted to tell him how I shoved someone I didn't even know, and how sometimes, I'm purposely late to class just so I can put off facing people for a few more moments. I thought about saying, "My gosh Carson, never complain? You obviously haven't seen my notebook! That's all I do!" But I didn't; I bit my tongue, knowing perfectly well I wasn't the epitome of a student he believed me to be, but I'd never convince him different.

    I've spent four years dreading each impending moment at that school. I've never once enjoyed my time there. There were moments when I laughed, but at the price of the tears and the blood in between... And in those four years, I've done nothing worthy of remembrance. I got myself pregnant... I left a bloodbath in the science room... Those are the things people are going to remember about me. It won't be for my writing, my music, how good my Psychology paper was, or how well-behaved I was. It's all going to be the things that I want to forget, and the halls of GCHS will never let that happen.

    I waited until my senior year, late in my senior year, to let the loneliness start to bother me to this level. I've done fine, even better, on my own until now. I've wasted a lot of opportunities to meet new people. All of the faces I see everyday are so sad to me, knowing that each person I pass in the hallway was a lost chance. And something I'm going to regret until the day I die is having lost the chance to form the relationships and the bonds I could have made there.

    Assuming I ever get to Murray, I'm not going to do what I've done at GC. I'm going to live the best that I can, and I know I'll be happy, knowing that I've left behind a bad legacy, and I have one more chance to try again. Even if life seems far too long now, I know it won't later. And I'm going to wish that I had made the best of the time God has given me to spend how I see fit.

Jessie

Where My Ink Comes From

<u>Sunday, March 22, 2009</u>
Dear Diary,
  It seems like these last couple of weeks have been my spiral. Between meltdowns in psychology class and shoving freshmen around, I haven't had much time for sanity. I've managed to sleep this entire weekend off and on, which hasn't been fair at all to my Dad and my Grandmother. Benjamin hasn't spent much time with me at all. And when he did, I felt like John Nash on *A Beautiful Mind* when the baby was crying, and he was too much of a zombie to do anything about it. I'm still exhausted, but at least I'm not too tired to halfway focus on things that actually matter. At this point, my music isn't making it on my priority list. I've got other things to worry about.

  I still have to pay my fees for MSU. I have to get my housing papers in, and portfolio deadlines are coming up... I don't have any more auditions for a while, and the school talent show hardly counts as anything important. I've changed my mind, anyway; I'm not signing up for that. I did, but I can back out anytime. I thought Brice was going
to do it too, but since he's not, I don't want to be the only one laughed at in Band. Although given the status of the performance, I might never have another chance to be heard... No, forget it. After all, it's 'Jesus music.' Isn't that what they call it?

  I have a theory; The last couple of weeks have brought out the worst in me. My inanity seems to reach its peak when I get in this place. I'm not going to stay in this place long enough to screw up again. I'm going to try to keep this week positive. Maybe if I do, I can get out of here. I'm going to get the sleep I need, not worry about music, and I'm going to let my notebook collect its dust. This week has to be better. I can't take another week like I've had to put up with.

Jessie

Monday, March 23, 2009
Dear Diary,

  I didn't see the need in paying more than the minimum when I won't be willing up very much. I just bought a journal with enough paper until I get up the nerve to do this.

  I could easily have died last night. I went into the bathroom with a razor more prepared than what I should've been. I had been reading about people who committed suicide, and relished in being able to relate to their sad stories that drove them to the end. As I read their stories, I thought about how much worse I was, and wondered why I had waited so long to join them. I even went so far as to read what Sylvia Brown said about suicide, just to ease the fear of facing God. I had the razor to my wrist, shaking, for a good half hour. What got me was that I wasn't afraid to die like I've been before. All that stopped me was Mamaw waking up.

  But the efforts weren't wasted. Now that I know I'm not afraid anymore, I can do this. It's just because... having made the decision to go through with this, I already feel better, like a huge weight has finally been taken off. I finally have the answer, and I can start to feel better. I have no obligations if I'm going to die; I can be happy, knowing what I do today will have no bearing on tomorrow. I feel invincible.

  Most of my notebooks have contained the sad stories of pathetic attempts; "I was so close," or, "I could easily have done it." My only regret is knowing that I won't have the pleasure of writing, "I was successful."

Jessie

Where My Ink Comes From

Tuesday, March 24, 2009
Dear Diary,

    I am so sick and tired of writing the same thing over and over and over again! And then to have everything I write lead to the same conclusion of me. I don't know what I expect when I hand the notebook over to Brice or Jones, like, "Here! I know you read this yesterday, but humor me." I get the same response every time; it's good. I KNOW it's good, or I wouldn't keep writing. My skills might be borderline mediocre, but at least it's art, and I don't know how to do anything else. Really, where would I be if I didn't have a pen in hand? What do I expect out of myself? I know my skills suck, but for someone like me, I think they're excellent. I'd laugh if I was someone else and come across my music, though.

    I'm just going to quit; I'm going to reply to Tamson's email, work on my play, gather up some research for my Spanish paper (because, you know, I don't plagiarize)... oh, that's another one...

    ...Never mind. My pen can't keep up with my mind, anyway...

                                                      Jessie

Saturday, March 28, 2009
Dear Diary,

    We had a scare today when band wasn't on next year's master schedule. Thank God, it was only a mistake, although it's still one that has me worried. I know what has been said, and I meant every word of it. Still, GCHS is the where I want my son to be when the time comes, and it's where I want to someday teach. It doesn't matter that I'm a senior; it's on everyone. I know I'm not the only one to pass through that band room and felt as though I had grown as a person for having done so. My only hope is that Gabriel will get to someday experience that, too.

    I finished my personal narrative last night. A couple of people wanted to read it, but I don't think it needs to ever see the light outside my altar again. Now, don't misunderstand. For once, I'm not saying that it's not good enough for anyone's time. Quite the opposite; I think it's TOO good. The details and the honesty 'C.N. King' was able to include makes it too personal for me to share.

Jessie

Saturday, March 28, 2009
Dear Diary,
    The only way I'm going to ever begin telling what I've been keeping to myself is to begin it straightforward. Any parts of my life that I deemed too painful to hold onto, the things that were completely unbearable, I never write about. It's my way of erasing the memories, and cleaning away the stain. Not that you guys can read this, but I'm very sorry for this. I wish I could share it, but I need to do this for me...

    ...I don't feel alright lately. I'm not sure what's gotten into me. I've never had the desire for my pain to end so badly, or the frustration to take a serious attempt on my life. I can't keep going on. I know I can't. But I don't understand... I don't want to die, but I feel like I'm supposed to. The narrative I wrote was so censored, even given how truthful it was. It was only a resolved version of a story still being lived and waiting on an ending. That ending may come too soon.

    I don't know how to explain it... I feel like I've truly reached the last days of my life. It's strange... I just don't see myself being here much longer. I keep having dreams that I'm beating on the cafeteria windows, trying to bring attention to the senior class reflecting on my death that I'm still very much alive. Last year, I had a similar dream, where I was playing my flute in the band room alone, and when Jones walks out of his office, I try to get his attention. In another scene, I see what he sees, and I'm not there. I remember thinking how I should be. I don't know why I have these dreams.

    I don't want to die. I have Benjamin to care for. But I still feel like something is going to happen to me, and I don't know why. I can't tell anyone, either. I'd be called crazy, if not suicidal, and sent away somewhere. Even given I don't want to die, I will. I'm not afraid to anymore, and I don't know what I'm waiting for. I don't think suicide will send you to hell when it's given as an option for dying. I just don't think so. And if I don't die, I'm just going to have to keep living, and I can't bring myself to keep living this life.

    Maybe the thing that caused me to want to end my life in the past is what is causing me to think this now. I've never felt as though I had anything to offer anyone. Any friends I've had, I've only hurt. I'll never forgive myself for what I did to Nora and Jamie, and I should consider myself fortunate that Cameron is even willing to breathe the same air as me. Brice and Daniel are soon to be the newest editions on that list of people that I've hurt, or that have hurt me. But both of them are so kind, more than what I deserve. I've had Daniel up until the morning hours, telling him about how pathetic my life is, and how unworthy I am of anyone's time and attention. Brice is a victim to the stories of desperate suicide attempts on nights when I couldn't see myself ever being worthy of life.

    I can't tell anyone the truth about the things that are

happening here in this house, or in my head. I'm certain I'd be considered insane. At worst, I'd be called a liar again, and I couldn't bear that. The events I had lied about would happen all over again, just so I would be reinforced in keeping my mouth shut. I can't let that happen again. My heart wouldn't take it.

I've just been going to school everyday now, hoping that someone will ask me what's wrong, and what is REALLY wrong. Not, "You can do it! Get your app and fees in," or, "You're such a good mom. Don't doubt yourself." Please, I just want someone to ask me if I'm alright, because I'm not. I'll be honest if they ask me. I promise I will be. The selfish part of me has forgotten that anytime I ask for help, I'm just a burden, and I need to stay quiet. The selfishness won't let me just go off alone to die. I'm too afraid. I want to give my life a fighting chance, even while this part of me is screaming that I truly deserve to be dead. But if I'm really meant to die here, nobody can do anything about it anyway, right? Even if I kill myself, this will just be where I die.

I must be insane to think these things now... God, what's wrong with me? When I die, I won't be saved. I've said the words in the past, and I tried to live life the best I could, but I could never find it in myself to have enough faith to believe that when I had truly reached the bottom of the pit, He would somehow reach down and pull me out like magic. I've come to believe in my time here that I was only proof that He makes mistakes. How could a God so loving ever create someone with a mind frame like I have and expect them to live in the world? It would make Him cruel. I don't understand.

There are a lot of things I can't wrap my mind around right now. The only thing I can say without apprehension of being wrong is that, no matter how strong my desire is to see the end of this place and the beginning of Murray, it may not be enough on that day that I have to get out the door with my son. People don't understand that their words of encouragement don't apply to me. They can't comprehend how truly dire that fight will be. I caused my dad's heart attack; even my cousin didn't try to argue with me when I told her that. I went on to tell her that I had no right to take his grandson away from him. I almost killed him the first time, and I wouldn't be able to live with myself if I ever caused another close call, or especially if that call didn't miss.

    I'd do this all night if I let myself. I'm not going to. I'm going to try my best to function this weekend, and try to find out what's caused me to lose my mind. I know I'm sick, but I'm not crazy. At least, I don't think I am. Not yet. But God, what am I going to do to get myself out of this one? It's always been my niche; to pull myself out of those dark corners when the need to had presented itself. Always having to be alone, I've learned to save myself all too well. Occasionally, I get in ruts that I don't see myself coming out of, but there was always that trace of hope that would allow me to continue on. Even in those suicide attempts, I wanted to live, or I wouldn't, have begged God to let me see another day when I thought I was dying. Before ever going after my wrist or downing any pills, it was always, "Jess, you know you're going to regret this, don't you?" And I did. I knew it, but in believing I owed a debt to society that I would never be able to pay, I thought that the only way I would ever come close would be to make sure I never hurt anyone again. I've since then come to learn that, even though I still feel as though I owe something, I really don't. It's been very duGCet to my mind's ear, but there are still so many other things about my life and my logic that I can't fix.

    The nagging fear in the back of my mind that everyday could be my last day with my son is driving me to insanity. I want the pain to end, not my life. I don't know what is making me feel so strongly that my time is limited now, unless it's knowing that I don't have the control anymore. It left with my sanity. I know that whatever happens, I'm going to attempt to make each moment with Benjamin count, beginning by shutting this stupid thing and lying next to him while he sleeps. Sometimes, I just lay there and watch him, overwhelmed with what can only be appropriately called a mother's love. That maternal instinct is all that makes me fear death now. And being as my cardinal trait is my own shyness and knowing how much of a burden I can be, I'm not allowed to fill anyone in. I just shut up and take it.

Jessie

<u>Sunday, March 29, 2009</u>
Dear Diary,

 I'm almost laughing looking back over my journal. It's gone from, "This last week has been horrible," to, "This last month has almost killed me." It's been over a month now that I began losing my mind. Days of being accused of plagiarism and being told how horrible of a mother I am, those easy days are gone, and I'm starting to miss them.

 It's frustrating to be where I am now, and I really can't explain how. An analogy... thinking... Like hearing nails on a chalkboard constantly. Frustration is fine when you know the problem will eventually be fixed, but I haven't reached the point of believing that yet. When I told Daniel about he music department nearly being cut last night, he said, "Believe in the magic," but isn't magic all about illusions?

 I think 'nails on a chalkboard' is perfect. I don't know how else to describe it. It's constant, and it's driving me crazy. The sounds of my own mind, I guess.

 Actually, reading back over this, I'm already crazy. But at least I admit it, unlike other artists. All writers are insane, they just keep it to themselves...

Jessie

Where My Ink Comes From

Monday, March 30, 2009
Dear Diary,
  The thought of cutting my wrist... only someone who has cut as long and as bad as me could understand. When a razor goes through your skin, you can hear it tearing you. The subtle sound is sickening to hear. I imagine that going through my wrist, a vein, and it's disgusting. I wish I could just die in my sleep and be done with it.

  I tried to last night. I tore at both wrists for well over an hour, and even went so far as to repeatedly go across the same wound. Except for that one, it just looks like I lost a fight with barbed wire. I felt so stupid. I kept cutting across the veins, and never got anything, even as hard as I was pushing. It felt like I could tear through bone. I eventually did dig around enough that I could see a vein, but the physical pain wouldn't let me go any further.

  The sun comes up to start my day again, and I'm left wondering why I let that chance slip away. Given that I only allow a small handful of people to read my music, people don't understand that my words are NOT just words; they're very literal. But no one cares. This is just God's way of telling me that this is meant to be my end. I'm supposed to die right here.

  I can't wait for this to all be over. Maybe if I'm lucky, God will pity me and let me run into a light pole before I get home from school.

                Jessie

Tuesday, March 31, 2009
Dear Diary,
   Sometimes at school, I'll think about calling home so I

can leave early and just do it. I start to think that I wouldn't back out if I were to do it at that moment, when I was feeling a bit braver. Ironically enough, I'm really not afraid to die. The actual process doesn't scare me, but not knowing what happens to consciousness, to the soul (assuming there is one), that's what scares me.

Do we choose to die? Is a near-death experience what you call it when you change your mind at the last second? The Bible is only a book of analogies... So is there really a heaven or a hell? Sylvia Brown said that we choose to come back here after reviewing in the Hall of Wisdom how we did. Sounds ludicrous, but is it? We don't have much to go by. God never just came out and said anything.

I'm not sure the thought of dying scares me nearly as much as the thought of living. I know that in two weeks from now, six months, a year, five years from now, I'm still going to be as screwed up as when I began. And I'd rather not be a part of something like that. If I haven't done something noteworthy by now, then I'm wasting my time and that of everyone else's in attempting. I've already done more than what I can ever make up for. The closest I'll ever come will be making sure that I don't bring anyone else down.

Would anyone be sad at all? I doubt it. If there's any sort of reaction at all, it'll be laugher over how stupid I am. They'll wonder why I didn't do it sooner, what took me so long. I think others would be glad, ecstatic that I'm gone. Still, there'll be plenty of people who don't care either way. The only tears at my funeral will be those of joy, far from grief. I know I'm not supposed to burden people. But as much as I've already done it, one more can't hurt much. I hate to be so weak, but I just want to tell somebody something before I do this. Jones is one of the people on my list to apologize to. Maybe I can talk to him; he'll laugh at me, and I'll be reinforced in my ideas. He'll tell me how stupid I am, and how I should suck it up and get over it.

I never want to hurt anyone, but I kick myself every time I let the chance to tell someone slip away. It's the egotistical part of me, begging my stronger half to tell someone my plans. I almost feel as though the real me is being held somewhere. And I'm in so deep, nobody can hear me cry for help. Who I really am isn't who I am now. Maybe this is finally the real me talking, because I don't want to do this. God, please don't let me die...

I wish someone could recognize that this isn't me, and I'm trapped. I'm not Jessie at all. Why can't someone see that? Because I conform to expectations. And nobody suspects anything at all out of someone who stays constantly in one place. To do anything would "come as no surprise." They would think that I was very ignorant. I think this one is particularly true, considering.

I can't stand this place anymore. I hate feeling like a military dog every time I walk into school. I hate what the school has become, with so many changes in my life there from last year. I hate being alone here all day long with no one to talk to. I'm tired of writing in bathroom stalls when I don't have anywhere else to go, people looking down on me, my obligations, everything. At home, I have to fight off my brother, and I pray that God forgives me for leaving Benjamin alone there. I'm a horrible mother. My son is so much better off without me.

I put a new razor in the bathroom, one not dulled by bad nights, for when something happens that compels me to go through with it. There have been a few occasions that I know I could've done it, but I never could find anything to do it with. I thought about drinking some tile cleaner one time, but even diluted in water, the burn on my lips was so bad, it scared me to think of that burning my stomach. I thought that it would be such a painful death. But with a razor, I won't need anything else.

But I still don't understand... why won't someone just ask me? I promise I won't lie, given I'm asked the right questions. But my standards are too high. No one cares, nor should they care. I'm as bad as they come, as ignorant and awkward as the two can get. I can't even speak right. Trying to talk to someone, they always look at me like they're trying to understand, and I know they don't. I stopped telling stories, and talking altogether. So it seems like who I was born as will be the cause of my death. I am my own demise.

Why would I go to hell for doing this? God makes faulty people who have no other choice, and we're just supposed to live life? God wouldn't make such sick people and then send them to hell for being ill. But what if it's caused by us? We cause our own lives, make our own beds, and that's where we lie, right? No. That still wouldn't make any sense. I don't understand this at all.

Constant frustration. Constant panic. Constant everything. It's reached the point that I can physically feel everything my mind has to offer. There's always a hook in my stomach or a burn in my chest, constantly. And no matter what I do, I can't shake it. I tried to make a list of all of the reasons that I had to live. Even if it seemed almost insignificant, it would still be worth adding. There wasn't one thing on that list; even my son is better off without me. I have no reason to live, but I have every reason to die. And the only reason I don't is because I'm a coward. But if I can ever get past the fear of what I don't know, I'll be gone.

People say that they can't get up in the morning, and I think how carelessly that phrase is tossed around. I've repeatedly brought new meaning to it. When I'm lying in bed in the morning before school, I hate myself even more, wishing that I had gone through with it the night before. I keep making that wish until, on some mornings, I'm driven to tears. When I say that I don't have the will to continue on, it's to the point where, at times, I stumble walking in the hallways at school because I don't feel like I can walk. In these places, I wonder what would happen if I just fell to the floor in tears. I know people would laugh at me, tell me to suck up and keep going.

    I'm not done yet. I have to keep going. I have to.

Jessie

<u>Wednesday, April 6, 2009</u>
Dear Diary,

    ...I can't say that I feel weaker after everything that happened today, but I can't say that I feel better, either. I'm not sure it did much for me, although I think it opened my eyes, somewhat.

    After band was out today, I talked to Jones for a little while on college issues. I told him that I wasn't sure about going, and that he couldn't possibly understand the fight that would happen the day I tried to leave. Immediately after telling him that I had been talking to Jamie about it, I got, "You've been talking to Jamie, and you're STILL worried?!" or something like that. Well, yes, I'm worried. I already know that college is a different world from high school, where ignorance isn't quite as obvious, and people are more tolerant to diversity of character. I don't have to be convinced of anything; it's my family that I have to get past.

    The only one that could ever begin to understand the reactions I'm going to get would be my mom. Just to paint a picture, let me say this... I will NEVER justify my mother leaving all those years ago. But now that I'm a mother, living with the same people as she did and having to do the same things she was forced to do... I understand it. I still don't think it was right at all, and never will, but I get it. And I have to say, I think she was amazing to have even tried. I have a little bit more respect for her just for her efforts. But I still blame her.

    I think the reason I'm so sick is because she was, too. And she passed those genes onto me. So being a bad mother may not be in my blood, but the reasoning behind it is. I know I can't be what Benjamin needs me to be, and I don't think I'll ever be able to.

I ran into Tamson at the store. I was hoping that she could just see it in me, that I wasn't happy at all. I wanted to tell her, and I think I would have, had I not been so keen at that time to stay strong. It's almost become a game for me, now. Nobody can know how unhappy I am, and I score a point each time I get away from people unscathed.

After I got home from school, I hung out with my cousin for a little while. I don't care if she is family, I needed socialization so much, particularly after today. The seclusion has really started to get to me lately. When she and her mom left and Benjamin went to sleep, I snuck off to go practice in the other house. With as little details possible included here, I'll leave it at... I wasn't happy. Finally telling someone that I was shying away from school because of the fear of disappointing everyone (just not exactly in those words) only reminded me of the deeper details.

After I got upstairs, my piano was on for five minutes before it was shut off. I did it without really thinking, and just said out loud, "I don't understand!" It wasn't the music, but my life; I was praying, for the first time in a long time. For a few weeks now, I would tell myself off and on that if this is as low as I can get, and I really don't have anything left to lose, what would the harm be in giving God a chance? But I immediately intermitted myself by saying that it wouldn't help, and I should waste my time or His. (One more reason my music is nothing but hypocrisy.)

I tried to shove off the urge to keep talking. But by then, I was shaking, and my thoughts were out of control. I was trying to play three notes over and over again, and the keyboard wasn't even on. So I quit, sighed, leaned back in the chair, and said it again. "I don't understand." I shook my head. "I really don't."

It's the truth... I really don't understand. Why should sin even exist when there are people like me whose options are limited? But is there anyone else like me, anyway? "Why did You put me in this house, knowing what would happen?" "Why did You let this happen to me?" "Stronger people could have handled this so much better." "I'm angry at You." "I can't find the faith to trust You." The fears and all the secrets I've been forced to keep lately, I let them come out, one right after another. At times, I wondered what would happen to me if someone walked in on me. They would know I was crazy, but I didn't care. I kept talking. I told Him every nasty secret I remembered at that moment. I talked about how sick I was and knew it, and how I couldn't even get help without being punished. My speech was disorganized; every story I needed to tell someone was scrambled, and it was like playing Pong in spilling my life's details out loud. And when my Dad knocked on the front door, I still hadn't said everything I wanted to.

By the time I heard the knocking, I was shaking and crying. I finally told Him the bottom line: If life has anything to offer me, I need to know what it is. Something is going to have to make itself known, because I can't take this anymore. I can't.

But then I thought... isn't this what I was thinking last year? And look where I am; worse off than I ever was. I was so stupid...

Jessie

Thursday, April 2, 2009
Dear Diary,

I failed my Spanish test today, miserably. I kept thinking that the test was on Friday, so I didn't study for it. What conjugations I did have were wrong, and I didn't even attempt the

-ar infinitive. By then, she knew I was an idiot, anyway. I had tried to do something with 'comer,' but I would have been laughed at all the way back to my seat if I had turned that in. Everyone had waited long enough on me trying to finish before they could talk, and all my stupidity was doing was holding them up. I felt so sick at one point, I felt like falling out of my desk. I finally did get up the nerve to turn my paper in, only to get, "Where are your sentences?"

Being the ignorant person that I am, I stuttered out something stupid. "...No..." "...I ran out of time..." "...I know. From yesterday...?" I couldn't even tell you what I said.

All this follows the worst highlight of the day... I asked Carson for an alternate assignment Tuesday after getting sick just thinking about presenting my Psychology project. He said that was fine, but when I got home, I felt guilty for asking. Everyone else had to do it, and I shouldn't have even asked. Besides, when I presented a PowerPoint sophomore year, it went alright, so this shouldn't have been any different. I told him today before heading to the library that I was going to do it, and he said that it was whatever I wanted.

After another student presented her project, Carson came over and asked me if I wanted to go ahead, or I could wait until tomorrow so I could have some practice time. But the Band is taking a field trip over to the middle school tomorrow to play for the students, so I didn't have much of a choice. It's spring break after that. So, feeling only slightly braver since standing up to my inner voice this morning, I stood up, went to the projector, and tried to pull my slideshow up. Immediately, I was wishing that I had stayed right where I was at.

I didn't last five minutes. Actually, that gives me too much credit; I didn't last half of one, even though it felt like an eternity. I broke down and said, "Can I do this tomorrow?" without even thinking that I wouldn't be there. But I think Carson knew better than to point out that fact, and just said okay. I logged off the computer and sat down, mortified and begging the earth to open up and swallow me. Carson came over to talk to me, but I was so torn up and shaking... I can't even remember what he said. I was just wishing he would go away, and not bring any more attention to the fact that I was a moron. I was supposed to be checked out early today for an appointment at the health department, and I was praying that my dad would hurry up and get me out of there.

    I laugh at the thought of me teaching a class of my own. I can't even look people in the eye when I talk to them, I'm so afraid. And I tried to present a PowerPoint? Much less obtain a teaching degree. If I end up having a miracle and going to college, I can't get into something that will have me working with people. I guess it would only be on God's good humor that someone with such an intense social phobia would fall in love with the idea of teaching. Then to add a cherry on top, I'm a musician. I don't know how to do anything other than my music, so how do you do either of those without involving people? You can't! So now, I'm not sure what I'm thinking.

    I'm stupid to not have thought of all this sooner. I should have known that I couldn't teach with the way I am. But it never even crossed my mind. As luck would have it, I wouldn't even find out that it wasn't an option for me until after I'd been accepted into MSU's Music Department for music education. So now, I'm completely lost. I centered the next forty years of my life on this, only to find out that I can't do it.

    ...What now?

    As hard as I prayed last night, I thought I would start to understand things better, see things clearer... I'm worse off than I was before.

    But isn't that the beauty of the whole situation? Sure, I'll be remembered as a very awkward social person, but that's just it; today won't influence tomorrow. I'll be gone soon.

Jessie

Friday, April 3, 2009
Dear Diary,
    There are times when I think about it, and it becomes very arduous to compose myself. After school yesterday, I went to the house that it happened in. It didn't look any different from what it did a year ago. I thought about just going into that room and trashing it. I wanted to set the bed on fire. I hate him so much! And I know that he could care less about what he's done to me, my life, my son's life... I'm paying the life sentence he deserves, and I can't tell anyone about it. I'm more alone now than I've ever been.

    God, I can still feel it. It was the most disgusting thing that's ever happened to me. He didn't care while he was doing it that it hurt. He was too caught up in talking to me. The last time I told him to stop, after I had been begging him to from the beginning, all he said was, "Just hold on! I'm almost done." He

had my hands down, so I turned my head, not wanting him to see that I was in pain. After he said that, I had tried to kick and get my arms loose for my last time. I just quit. I wanted it to be over so badly, I didn't try to fight him anymore. And after he was done, all I got was, "I really wish you hadn't given into me. I'm sorry. Don't make it so easy next time."

    I hate him! I've never hated anyone so much! Even being in the same room with him makes me sick. But he was right; I made it too easy for him. It was my fault. I wasn't raped. I must've wanted it, or I could have proven that I didn't by trying harder to get away. There were people nearby that could have heard my screaming if I had only summoned the courage to do so. But I just wanted it to end. And because of my selfishness, because I gave up, I'm paying for it. I got pregnant, and I can't tell anyone that I'm not the slut they imagine me to be. I was never with anyone. Daniel asked me one time if I was sure that who I thought was the father really was. I knew he had to ask, but I still wondered if it might've been because I came off as someone who would sleep around. If I do, nobody is going to believe me. They wouldn't have, anyway.

I sat in a swing watching the window of the room. No one was home, and maybe I shouldn't have been there, but I didn't care at the time. I stared at the room, wanting to do something, but I still don't know what. Destroy it, maybe. Destroy him. Destroy myself. The whole house was a harsh reminder. Driving past it in the morning turns my stomach. I hate that place. I'll never go back there, not alone. I can't.

Jessie

<u>Friday, April 3, 2009</u>
Dear Diary,

Jeremy IMed me today. I don't want to talk about it. To cut the long story short, I was called a whore, told that nobody gives a flying fuck about me, and was given a strong recommendation to put my son up for adoption. I called Brice out of desperation, hoping maybe he could do damage control after he said he was going to post the conversation publicly. I should've known better that to believe it, anyway; I, after all, never once insulted him in any way. Anytime it was my turn to reply, all I said was, "Anything else?" He took me off his friends list in mid-conversation, so I couldn't access the note he said he was going to post. That's where Brice came in.

I love Brice. I called him and told him to get on

facebook. And after a discussion on how right Jeremy was (and Brice, of course, trying to convince me that he wasn't), I broke down and told him. I admitted that I really wanted to die.

omg really
go to the doctor
please Jessie
don't do this

      The bargain was, I go to the doctor Monday and see what he says, or Brice was going to his dad (who, by the way, was former vice principal, and happens to work at the school board now). I knew if he did that, I'd be shipped off somewhere, so I guess I'm going to the doctor Monday. It won't matter. I'm still going to die. If I don't die, I'm going to continue on like this, and I can't go through life anymore with things how they are now. I can't change how I feel, even if I could turn back time. I'm so sorry, Brice.
      The difference between contemplation before and now is that before, I always saw another way out. As long as I held to myself enough and toughed it out, I always came out fine. Now, my life has been destroyed beyond repair, and I'm going to be someone's mother for the rest of my life. I love Benjamin, but I'm going to hurt him more than I help. And unlike before, I'm angry enough to do it. I've never known how strong hate could be until now, now that I've admitted everything to myself. And I'm angry enough, I hate him enough, that the emotions are enough that I won't center a plan on anyone finding me. This is the one time that I can say, beyond a doubt, I'm ready.

                                                                         Jessie

Where My Ink Comes From

<u>Saturday, April 4, 2009</u>
Dear Diary,

    The bed was lying out on the lawn last night. It was the same bed that started everything. I guess it was thrown out for the springs, because it was turned upside down, and it looked pretty torn up underneath. And I lost it.

    After dragging it into our yard, I ran back into the house and grabbed my Dad's jug of coal oil and matches. The writing of 'burn the bed' from my notebook was flashing bright, sounding itself in my mind. I threw the oil on the bed, lit a piece of trash nearby to throw on, and it engulfed itself in only a few moments. I watched it burn for a long time, afraid to leave it for the neighbors that might call the fire department if it was burning without anyone nearby. I watched the flames, feeling a sense of happiness for the first time. I felt vengeance, or at least a degree of it. I was crazed, but I didn't feel insane. I only felt happy watching the bed burn. I remember thinking, this is where it happened, and this is where it ended.

    When I went into my dad's house, I fell on the couch. I was so scared sitting there. What I didn't want to admit, what I wanted to take to my grave, was killing me. And immediately, I was overtaken at the thought of my disgrace. Here I was, waiting for someone that wasn't coming, who I knew in the back of my mind wouldn't come... Even looking back on it makes me feel crazy. I can see myself in third-person, and I didn't look good. Something else came to mind in those few moments of that realization too: He won. He wanted me to be afraid of him, and I was. He won.

    I spoke out loud without thinking. I didn't care if anyone heard me or not. If I had been there with someone, I don't think it would have changed what I did next. I asked God why He had let this happen to me, and why no one could help me. I could never bring myself to say the words that really needed to be said. I could go on and on in my journals, my stories, my music, and I would keep repeating myself until I told the truth.

As angry as I was with God at that time, I did say one thing to Him during that hour-long prayer that wasn't antagonistic. "I need You."

I did need Him. I was angry, hurt, everything I had every right to be, but it wasn't God that I was enraged with.

"I need You."

And I do.

                Jessie

Sunday, April 5, 2009
Dear Diary,

In my frenzy, I forgot to close shop. My Dad nearly had another heart attack when he found the huge pile of ashes in our backyard, his jug outside, his front door wide open, and the keys in the door. He asked me what I had tried to burn, and my reply was ignorantly, "I forget now what it was." He told me to never ask for the keys to his house again, because I wasn't allowed back over there without him. Of course, after he had said it, I wanted to kick myself for leaving things that way. I don't know why I didn't think to do the obvious.

My family has been complaining about how little time I spend with Benjamin, and how I need to stop writing so much and play with him more. My journal keeps me sane; I could never give it up. Maybe it'll pay off someday...

                Jessie

Monday, April 6, 2009
Dear Diary,

I didn't go. I don't know what Brice is going to say. If he

Where My Ink Comes From

doesn't ask, I'm not bringing it up. I just couldn't do it. What if I go in there and the doctor ships me off somewhere? That's what they do with people like me. Even a hint of what I'm planning, they don't give you any chances.

    I got a letter from Murray State University today, congratulating me on being a new member of the Racer Band. Looks like I've been officially accepted. It's small, but it's a start. A start is a lot more than I've had so far.

                                                  Jessie

Tuesday, April 7, 2009
Dear Diary,

    Benjamin had a wonderful day (sarcasm at its best). Not three hours after tripping with him over his walker and scaring him half to death (which, ironically enough, had 'Safety 1^{s}' printed on the front), he wiggles himself out of my lap, and... onto the floor. He flew out of my arms, and had I not been sitting down and in the living room where he landed on the carpet, he might've been hurt. I've never heard him cry like that, even when I tripped. That one got me, and I ended up with a nasty gash.

    This is the downside of what I do. Occasionally, it just gets really bad, and I end up with a worse scar than usual. You already know this. I had a new razor, and typically, mine are only a smidge dull from light use. So, I've learned a new lesson today: In cases of extreme distress, DON'T use a new razor. New blades are abnormally sharp, and your emotions can drive you to press way too hard. After you've been doing this for a while, you tend to notice things. One of those things is how to accurately understand the extent of the damage done, or the depth of the injury. If it takes several seconds for a hint of blood to ever appear, you've done an excellent job, one that will bleed a lot in time. Amateur cuts tend to bleed immediately. I'll give you a guess at which one I had.

It was gaping, and hurt so badly. It bled horribly before I finally got some butterfly bandages on it. I have to turn to those when I need stitches I know perfectly well I'll never get. I closed the wound, but when I took the band-aids off tonight after my shower, it came back open and bled even more than earlier. I couldn't keep it closed, so I wrapped it in tape and gauze, and I'm hoping it stops bleeding before morning. I'll get sick if I bleed too much. I have iron pills that I take for when this happens, but it takes them a couple of weeks, at best, to work and get me back up to par. In the meantime, I'll be persistently tired.

Jessie

Friday, April 10, 2009
Dear Diary,

I had a comforting thought today. And I can honestly say that this is probably the greatest revelation I've ever had.

Jesus was born of a virgin. But when Mary turned up pregnant, all anyone cared about was, "You're not married!" And of course, who was going to believe that she had never had sex? How could Joseph believe that? So Jesus was automatically born by sin, 'cause everyone assumed. He was doomed right from the start.

Jesus was hated by everyone. They all called Him a liar, a sinner... everything but the kitchen sink, basically. Even his own disciples from time to time thought He was nuts. He was by Himself a lot, praying, thinking, whatever He felt like doing at that time, I guess. Jesus was absolutely perfect; all-around, no mistakes, the epitome of a man, because he wasn't a man at all; He was God. He was despised to the point that people wanted Him gone, and they made Him suffer a horrible death. And all He ever did was help people; cured people of their illnesses, and made miracles happen.

    I was thinking about this for a song idea, and it hit me; my revelation. And that revelation was... me and Jesus had a lot in common.

    I don't know if it's something that shouldn't be said, but it's the truth. I thought of something else, too. Even though Jesus was hated by everyone, lonely, tried to be perfect, knew He was going to be crucified for the things He had done, He still did. And even while He was hanging by the nails on the cross, He had faith in God. He knew He had nothing to fear, even though the world had turned Him down.

    There is one difference, though; I'm not perfect. Jesus was. And if He was perfect and still didn't win, how can I even try and expect to come out on top? I have scars lining my arms beyond what anyone could ever imagine without seeing, and a past that's far from perfect. I tried to do my best, but it was never good enough. All I did was hurt people. But my thought did prove a point; if Jesus couldn't win, I should've known better than to even try.

                                                           Jessie

<u>Sunday, April 12, 2009</u>
Dear Diary,
    I haven't had the computer in the last week or so to write anything. My Dad kicks me off every time, saying, "Check my email. Did she write back?" He signed up for an online dating

thing because he broke up with Sue for the fiftieth time, and went and sent the website a money order so he could have all the features for a month. But he's computer-challenged, so he sits down next to me and has all these commands. "Check my email!" "Write her!" "Check her profile." "No, she's too fat." "Stop flipping it!" And to make it worse, he doesn't understand how a computer works at all. So he thinks that I'm always doing something on it wrong. He always goes back to Sue though, so this won't last long.

    Benjamin's first Easter had much to be desired. He's been sick the last few days. Running a fever, coughing, etc. So I guess he's going to the doctor tomorrow. That'll mean no school for me. My Grandmother thinks that they can't take him to the doctor, that I have to be there. I really don't. Every time he gets a runny nose, they think he has to get an antibiotic. They did that to me, and now I can't get over a cold at all. I had one in late February, and I still can't breathe through my nose. It's ridiculous. And I don't want Benjamin to have his immune system destroyed with that stuff like me.

    My Easter, on the other hand, was fun. I haven't colored eggs in a good decade, or so. I did last night for Benjamin (claimed that it was for Benjamin, anyway). I made some with words on them, others had stickers, and some had plastic wraps and stripes. I even went out of my way to punch the props out and I put them on display so that everyone would see them when they woke up. I wish I could see Benjamin paint his first Easter eggs when the time came, or open his first birthday or Christmas present, or eat his first slice of turkey at Thanksgiving. I hope I'm strong enough to stick around and see those things for myself.

                                                                  Jessie

Monday, April 13, 2009
Dear Diary,
    I'm actually pretty glad that spring break is over. I barely know what to do with the weekends, let alone an entire week to myself. I have to have my order. Being in school provides me with somewhat of a schedule to follow. I have to be honest; I don't like change. Another reason I'm dreading graduation.

    I got my housing papers off for MSU, by the way! Sweet. And I got kicked out of the band room. Durnham walked in there with a police officer looking for the gym coach (don't ask, I don't know). And after I told her I wasn't sure where he was if he wasn't in the gym, she said, "Where's Jones?" Again, I told her I wasn't sure, maybe in the lounge. "Where are you supposed to be?" Child Development class. But hey, I'm only a mom, so I should probably be in class, since I don't know anything about it. It was obvious that I was up to something mischievous as I sat there at the piano playing my scales. "Why are you in here?" I'm waiting for you to leave so I can pop out the whiskey. No, I told her I was going to Murray, and I had to learn certain scales. Truth. TRUTH. "A teacher should be in here with you." Oh, really? So when Jones came back, scared I had gotten him into trouble, I started to ask if he ran into her. He just told me I had to go back to class, because I had been seen.

    God, I miss Mr. Reynolds so much. If that had been him, or even Brice's dad, he would have asked how the band was going, my college plans. (Well, maybe not on that particular occasion, if they were doing something with a police officer and a teacher, but that's beside the point.) I miss everything that our school was last year. Our new administration is making enjoying our senior year really, really hard.

    At least in getting back to school, I didn't procrastinate. Within the first four classes, I'd already written two songs, and had started a good idea for a third one. The first two were okay, but I'm really, REALLY looking forward to this one! It's going to be based off a previous analogy I've used... when I said Jesus and I had a lot in common. And I can, rest assured, say that this has never been done before! Every songwriter's dream is to write what no one else has thus far.

Jessie

Tuesday, April 14, 2009
Dear Diary,

    We're having a band banquet for the first time. It's on a Tuesday night, the night my dad works, so I probably won't get to go. I can't call up people I know for rides like everyone else can when I don't have anyone. And Sunday, I got my hair cut. I have bangs now, and a little bit of layers. I don't look as much like a twelve-year-old anymore. I don't have anyone to walk with at graduation, so I'm not going to. I went in the high school playing my music, and I'll leave doing the same thing. How many seniors can say they played their own *Pomp and Circumstance*? What else...? I went to see Madison for my yearly check-up yesterday. I can't believe it's been a year since I was in her office listening to a second heartbeat. I got my confirmation letter that I'm now in MSU's racer band, and I have an official Murray State email address. I broke my two-and-a-half year-old glasses, super-glued them, and finally got tired of waiting on my grandmother to make me an appointment for the optometrist. She didn't want me to make it; she wanted to wait until everyone could go together, but I have to go above her sometimes.

    Oh, but the worst... Remember that story Daniel suggested I write? I saved it on my jump-drive, not on the computer, so that I would know for sure that no one could see it but me. It was stolen at school. I don't want to even think about someone reading that. I didn't even get to read it. I'm still in a bit of a panic, but on the plus side, I saved it as a hidden file. Brice said that someone ignorant enough to steal from someone else isn't going to be smart enough to know how to pull it up. I hope to God he's right, but... ...Worse, I'm never going to get up the nerve to write anything even remotely similar to that again.

And to the present, we had our band concert tonight. This was our last one (for seniors). We had that stupid thing where we, the seniors, had to stand after Jones talked about us, and something he said is still ringing in my mind. I went first, and he said, "She's had to overcome a lot." I don't even remember what else he said, because I was too focused on that (and the fact that he wanted me to stand up and draw attention to myself). It was just a sad reminder. It's been five years, and I haven't gotten past a thing, even though everyone gives me credit for having done so. My problem is, I'm never going to change. And walking off the gym floor for the last time only reminded me once again that I've wasted so many chances. If I had given GC half the chance it deserved, I would have been such a better person. I would have had friends, good memories, and less embarrassing ones. But it looks like as of now, my opportunity is over.

I made an idiot out of myself tonight, to add insult to injury. The seniors wanted to take a group picture, and of course, I didn't want to be in it. Daniel is in charge of our class Senior Video, and he's determined to get everyone at school in the picture. And they kept saying, "It's for Daniel! He ASKED us to make sure you were in it! Do it for Daniel!!!" And I did it, but not for Daniel. I was tired of looking stupid, and they would remember my ignorance, anyway. They wouldn't need a picture. So now, they have this embarrassing photo of me looking down at the ground, and with this horrible hair cut, I probably broke the camera, and it's going to be put on a video for everyone to see. Thanks, Band...

It was the longest concert we've ever played. We started at seven o' clock , and we didn't get finished until eight forty-five.

It was pretty bad. Yet, to make matters even worse, we had to play 'Under the Sheets,' also known as *Under the Sea*. I still don't understand why Jones put us through such torture, but why not?

    Jones announced tonight that Cameron got accepted into Governor's School for the Arts. Brice got alternate. I'm happy for them both. It hurts, reminding me of how I didn't get to go and bring that glory home to anyone. Not that anybody really cared at the time, but I did. Anyway, I'm just glad that Cameron is going to get to represent Green Central in that environment, and Brice will get to do it even better next year.

Jessie

Saturday, May 2, 2009
Dear Diary,

    To explain my absence... I'm not sure I know exactly what I'm doing anymore. I guess I should be glad for it, but I can't be. Truth be told, I'm so used to being worried, hurt, upset, distraught over something, that not only do I manage to hide it perfectly well, but I've taught myself to manage it. But this, now... this is new. Now, I'm at a point where I'm nothing. I wouldn't even say that I was numb. I'm just... indifferent, I guess. And I have nothing to say.

    I saw Mandy yesterday, and it tore me apart. She was at school to sit in on classes as part of her teaching degree. A part of me, for a split second, had the thought of breaking down right there in front of her in tears and telling her everything, and I would have if I thought I could tell her what happened. But I knew better than to do that, so I bit my tongue. I would have felt stupid. At one point, I just looked at her, smiled, and looked down at the ground. I started to say, "You have no idea how glad I am that you're here." I don't know why I didn't say it, but now she'll never know. I just can't wait to get to Murray and be with them all again.

Jessie

Saturday, May 2, 2009
Dear Diary,
  I love Daniel. I can honestly say, no one has really been able to say the words I need to hear quite like he has. It seems like he's the first to make a radical difference in my life. Yet, he needed someone tonight, and I couldn't be it...

  Daniel writes articles for our local newspaper. (He's such an amazing writer, and I will never understand why he doubts that.) He has basically given up the better half of his life to the Green Ledger, sacrificing his homework and social life for it, but when it came time to give the job of editor out, they didn't give it to him. They gave it, instead, to someone who has barely worked there a month. How could they? I don't know how good of a writer she is, but I'd put money on Daniel to go up against any author out there. He said it broke his heart, and I didn't have the words to help him.

  I don't remember what I told him now. He said he felt like he had lost his pen (he considers his pen to be his voice, so the two are the same to him) and I said something stupid like, "You haven't lost your pen. I'm reading you loud and clear. When you actually do lose your pen, we'll look for it." And I mentally kicked myself for sending him such a stupid message. He said in the end that I did help him, but I don't think I did very much at all. I'm sorry, Daniel...

  ...I know, one day, I'll be able to say the words that people need to hear. I'm horrible with them now, but the day will come. Hopefully, it's not long off that my writing, my music, the words behind them, can inspire and heal. It's a nice thought, even if it is a far dream to have.

Jessie

<u>Monday, May 4, 2009</u>
Dear Diary,

  Our graduation has not changed for 25 years. Every year, it's been graduates walk in, parents sit behind them, and the band in the very back. Durnham, at a teachers meeting, asked when teachers wanted to walk in. According to our English teacher, she asked, "Walk in? We've never done that!" And Durnham just told her that we were going to do it now, and to direct any complaints to her. But when anyone has gone in her office, she tells us that it was the teachers' idea. No teacher we've heard from wants to walk, much less suggested it. So if we're going to get lied to, how do we fight it? Students have been in an uproar all day. When I asked Carson about it, he was outraged that Durnham would tell us that it was teacher-initiated.

  Carson said, "Jessie, my son has a tournament to go to every year, and I don't go to graduation. Will you be disappointed?"

  I told him no. I don't feel as though any teacher has let me down in the four years I've been at Green Central. And if a teacher can't take pride in seeing their students walk in a cap and gown from the sidelines, then something is wrong with the way they're teaching.

  "I've stood behind you all year, Jessie. I don't need to stand behind you at graduation to prove that."

  Well said.

Jessie

Where My Ink Comes From

<u>Wednesday, May 6, 2009</u>
Dear Diary,

I hate Durnham! I hate our new principle, and I hate what this school is becoming! The new administration with its changes is tearing our school down brick by brick, and the students are just watching it happen. Who's going to stand up to them?! Does anyone even care that this is our home, and it's being destroyed?

Diary, I couldn't believe it. Durnham passed out pink slips to teachers. Mrs. Venson was telling some students about it before lunch, and I happen to overhear. Four teachers; I thought I heard Mrs. Holly. I knew I didn't, and I asked Venson about it on my way out to the library (I can go there now; no more bathroom novels). I told her that I knew it was none of my business, but that I wanted to make sure I heard her right.

"Did I hear you say that Holly got a pink slip?" I thought my heart stopped when she nodded. Holly, the English teacher who didn't give up on my writing when I had given up on it my freshman year; the same English teacher who believed in me, and didn't laugh at me like most teachers do at everything that comes out of my mouth. She cared about my words when I couldn't share them with anybody else.

How on earth could Durnham do this? And why did I have the audacity to even ask and confirm my fears? What did I expect her to say after hearing the conversation for myself? "No, you heard wrong. Holly will be here forever." What was I expecting? I wish she would've lied.

…Holly, two of my math teachers, and two of my science teachers… I just need to know why. I have news for Durnham; Howell, my freshman math teacher, was all our math department had going for them. And Christiana, one of the science teachers, WAS the science department. How stupid is our principle? How soon until she fires Jones? Gets rid of the music department altogether? I had wanted to come back here and teach, but all today showed was that I may very well work for four years to find out that I'm not weGCome back to where I came from. I won't be weGCome

Diary, you weren't around my freshman year when I was caught with a razor at school, but Holly stuck by me. When I was taken to the conference room in the office to be bandaged up, she was there running her hands through my hair, speaking softly when everyone else was loud and alarmed from never having dealt with someone like me before. She wasn't scared; she knew me. She knew that I wasn't going to hurt anyone else when I was the only one I hated. Before that, we weren't that close, but I stayed in her room as much as possible when I was facing the ridicule of being back at school with classmates who didn't understand. She listened, every time I needed someone to. I couldn't talk to Holly today, but seeing how upset she was last year when she only thought she was going to lose her job, I worry. I hope she's alright.

Durnham has robbed the incoming students at GCHS of a wonderful opportunity to have her, all of them, as teachers. And I'm so sorry for those students. I'm sorry for myself and for Daniel, when we had hoped for the honor to work alongside them one day as educators. I hate Durnham.

When we got to Band today, Jones held his hand up above his head and said, "This is shitty," he lowered his hand and added, "and this has been your senior year. I'm so sorry, seniors…"

I am, too.

Jessie

Friday, May 8, 2009
Dear Diary,
	I've been talking to Shelby lately. Remember, from my Child Development class, whose mom came to talk to us about domestic violence? I've moved seats in Spanish, and I've been talking to her a bit. Another girl, Allyson, is in my first period and Spanish, both. It's nice to have somewhat of a social life outside of facebook now. I can talk to them both. I can't believe I didn't mention them before, but it seems like life is slowly, slowly changing, not fast enough for me to take note right off.
	Here's something else you'll never fathom. Diary, I can't quite wrap my mind around it yet, but it's been two whole weeks; no new scars. I hadn't even noticed. Time seems to be speeding up, going too fast for me to keep up with, but that's meant in the best way possible. Maybe it's been Shelby and Allyson, Daniel and Brice, and having someone to share a general conversation with. I don't feel so lonely anymore. I'm not sure if I need to say this now or wait until I know for sure, but… I feel better. Somehow, something is different. I can't put my finger on exactly what it is, but it's a weGCome change.
						Jessie

Sunday, May 10, 2009
Dear Diary,
	Daniel, as much as I love him, has incuGCated one idea in me that I still can't decide is good or bad. This might change tomorrow, but for right now, it's bad… At least, it was. Rewinding…
	…Today, I gave Mr. Carson the paper I wrote a couple of nights ago. It was about what happened between me and Jamie.

The details were gruesome enough with just me, but I talked a bit about her life experiences, too. I shouldn't have given it to him. I didn't have Jamie's permission. I felt bad about it, so now he's going to learn the dark secrets of two people. Not that Jamie's was all that dark. She's too happy all the time to have much wrong with her. But Carson is a writer. I've been relying on Daniel too much lately. Just because he's there doesn't mean I have to use him. He does have a life outside of my writing, after all. And Holly, with all the other English teachers, is knee-deep in portfolio deadlines, and I would feel bad for asking her to help. Coleman was there and readily available, so he got it. I trust him, so it's not that. I just worry about what he will think of me when he reads about my "razor fetish," as Jamie used to call it. So I went to Daniel anyway, needing a reassuring word. And trust me, that grammar dork knows a LOT of words...

...I owe a great portion of my story to Daniel; my life story. We've often talked about how much he's done for the school, and how the thinks that he didn't do enough with the four years he had at GC. He doesn't think his words, or his pen for that matter, is of any use at all. Daniel, if only you knew...

For some reason, I couldn't believe the words I heard from others. Mary, Jamie, Jones, and Mandy all used to tell me how valuable I was, and how much I was needed and loved. They used to tell me that the day would come when I would be okay, but I couldn't believe it. I never felt as though the words of inspiration, the 'be strong' speeches, or even the Bible could apply to me, because I thought God had forgotten me. Like I said, my only purpose was to prove that God wasn't perfect. I didn't even feel like I was meant to be born. I don't know what has made Daniel so different, but his words were fathomable. It wasn't even that the things he said were all so different from the things others have said. Maybe it was knowing who he was as a person; sincere, honest, and dedicated to his school and writing. There's something about his personality that makes it very easy

Where My Ink Comes From

for me to believe him.

Daniel believes in me. Thank God, because nobody else does. I certainly don't have faith in me, but I have faith in his words. And if he thinks I'm going to leave my mark on the world, then I'm just going to have to do it his way. He told me once that he had been inspired by me, and I believed it. I don't know what I did, but I must've done something right. He told me that I was going to earn a title for my name. He must really have faith in GC's students to believe in one like me.

I hope I'm not speaking for myself too early, but... It seems like I'm so much happier now than I used to be. Happy isn't a good word, because I'm really not. But I don't have that constant ache inside like before, or that sense of hopelessness and uselessness that I had accepted would just be a part of my life. I don't feel so numb anymore, or so faint. Before Daniel sent that message that began out friendship, I was barely holding myself up. I was holding onto my life by a thread. But something Daniel did instilled a desire in me to live. Conversely, it might've been a fear of death he instilled, the fear of dying without having earned a title worthy of remembrance. When I die, I'll completely disappear, and my name will be whatever people wish it to be. I can't give people that chance.

Maybe it was Daniel's fallacy of deeming himself unsuccessful that drove him to chase so much. His flaw turned out to be his greatest tool. He's a perfect example of what I should do; use my shortcomings and my deficiencies to make something beautiful happen for me, just as he has with his writing; his deficiency being his confidence, leading him to strive for a good writing. Maybe it was his pride, his humility, or his faith in God that compelled him to pursue my mental health, but I think it just boils down to... ...Daniel is a good kid.

Diary, do you remember a long time ago, and I said that if God couldn't fix me, then nobody could? I think God took that as a dare. And I think... that maybe He sent Daniel to prove me wrong.

                                                          Jessie

<u>Thursday, May 14, 2009</u>
Dear Diary,

      Spanish class today was truly the greatest time I've ever had in any class. And it was in the class that I hate the most... maybe not the most, but it's at the bottom of my list. Venson has a pink flamingo in her room, and it's been there since my freshman year, anyway. I'm sure it's been there longer. Dylan, the class clown, was acting up with it, and he tried to wrap the flamingo's legs around his head. I blinked and missed what everyone was laughing at, but when I finally saw what was happening, Dylan had torn the flamingo's foot OFF! Not torn, but ripped it OFF. Completely off. Everyone was laughing, and Dylan was trying to set it back on the shelf in a way that it looked like he was still attached. Someone said, "Awww, he looks so sad now that he lost a foot." And he did, making me laugh even harder.

      Venson, during this entire incident, was outside with a girl doing an oral test. When she same back in, most of us had tears in our eyes from laughing so hard, me included. And when she was trying to decide who to give the test to next, Dylan said, "Break a leg," and we all cracked up again.

      Venson said, "You guys aren't telling me the full story."

      I thought I was going to lose it when another girl said, "While you were gone, Dylan told us a story about nearly breaking his leg trying to wrap them around his head." Her face when she was saying to say that got me more than what she said, because she got to 'them,' and was laughing so hard, she was silent and couldn't finish her sentence.

      I will always remember today. Every time I look at a flamingo...

Where My Ink Comes From

In all seriousness, it was wonderful, for those few moments, to forget about my life and laugh at the good events in it for a little while, even if that little while was very short. And I think that's why, on the way home from school today, there was a short moment where I thought about the rest of my life... and I got excited about it. It didn't last very long, but it still happened. The fact that it happened should be enough of a step in the right direction.

I just have to decide now if I want to stray away from the shelter I've built, or try to keep going. This shack's about to blow away anyway, and the ship might be gone by the time I decide I want to jump on it. If I jump now, I might have a lot of days like today, or a lot of nights like before, where I end up playing a classic game of Slice-and-Dice. What's it worth to me? What's my life worth to me, that I'm willing to fight for it? Is it worth anything at all?

Jessie

Saturday, May 16, 2009
Dear Diary,

I'm getting sick. It always begins with a sore throat...

...On a happier note, I got new glasses today. And I made an appointment for this Monday for contacts. I've always wanted them, and this new eye doctor is so much cheaper than my last one. The one I was waiting on my grandmother to call was going to charge just under $300 for everything the last time I had asked him. This doctor, Dr. Ward, charges $30 upfront, and that pays for any number of visits it takes, the contact trial pairs, the whole nine yards. I won't have to pay for anything again until I get my actual contacts.

I wrote more music today. Benjamin held his bottle and put himself to sleep tonight. Gosh, he's adorable... And I'm at three weeks. I couldn't even tell you where my razor is. Things are getting better, Diary. I can feel it...

Jessie

Thursday, May 19, 2009
Dear Diary,

    Our Spanish and Psychology final was today. I don't think I did horrible on the Spanish, but I wasn't so sure how Psych was going to go. I used my exemptions that I got from testing for both, but went ahead and took them both, anyway. Venson requires that we take it, but Carson doesn't. Regardless, when you exempt either one of them, both teachers will only add it to the grade book if it helps you. If it hurts, they throw it out. Not that I could use my exemptions for anything else (Jones refuses to take any kind of exemption, since our finals are our concerts). Carson, as I was leaving, said, "Good job on the final today." I asked him if I had done that good, and he said, "I think you had about the highest in the class."

    Diary, do you realize what he said? "Best in the class..." I've never done that before! If I passed a test at all in any class, I was extremely fortunate. I just freeze up on tests, get nervous, and forget everything I've studied in advance. And unlike Venson's final where we could use our notes, books, and dictionaries, Carson's final flew solo.

    I'm going to feel really stupid if everyone did badly on the test, and I just got the highest failing grade, though...

    I've mentioned this often enough before, but... I can picture myself doing something in the Psychology field. I would never want to be a therapist, or anything like that. It'd be nice to break away from this label of a musician that everyone has on me. I've been doing some research on careers offered in the field, and you would be amazed at the number of options. There are cognitive psychologists, school psychologists, social psychologists, rehabilitation psychologists, research psychologists, experimental psychologists, art, sports, and even music therapists! Everything imaginable is offered. It would be a far cry from my music, but something about the class has intrigued me this year. It's nothing like what I thought it would be, and I'm really glad I took the class instead of the alternative of archaeology. I thought about talking to Carson to see what he suggested as far as careers and career research, but I've been spending too much time in his room as it is. I like talking to him, too. He, like Holly, is one of very few adults who doesn't laugh at me.

Jessie

Wednesday, May 20, 2009
Dear Diary,
  ...I've been thinking...
  ...We were assigned to read *Night* for my English class, and I just finished it not long ago. It was a portrayal of the holocaust by someone who survived a concentration camp.
  Elizer, as he's called in the book, watched as families were separated to the left and to the right. He and his father went left, his mother and sister right. They were all hauled into separate cattle cars, and Elizer and his father ended up in a camp in Birkenau. Those considered useless for work were sent to the crematorium there to be burned. Elizer was fifteen, too young to work, and his father was fifty, too old to work. A guard told them to be eighteen and forty, without telling them the reason why was so that they wouldn't be killed. Elizer watched bodies turn to smoke, with the guards having drawn no lines to cross. Babies

were brought in by truckloads to be thrown mercilessly into the pit of fire, just the same as old men were. For the guards' own sick amusement, the Jews were forced to march to crematorium, and then turned around again, just to make them think that they were going to be killed.

Elizer was a very pious teenager before being captured. Yet, upon seeing these things, be began to hate God. Physical pain overpowers mental anguish when there's enough of it. Even so, Elizer and the other Jews were beyond being broken. With the weight of their heavy hearts, they were starved, beaten, overworked; they watched their families be murdered, and their children be raped. They watched scenes unfold that were the most atrocious possible to be manmade. After a certain point, their broken minds didn't think anymore. Fathers turned against their own sons for just crumbs. They cared only about a ration of soup and some bread. The dead and dying lining their paths were envied.

Elizer lived. His father didn't.

Elie Wiesel, the author and survivor, received the Nobel Peace Prize in 1986, and his speech is written in the back of the book. Near the end of his speech, he said, "Our lives no longer belong to us; they belong to all those who need us desperately." My son needs me. Who else will protect him? No one else knows his father; the perverse monster that he is keeps me awake at night. Thank God that, besides being irrational, unpredictable, and crazy, he was also a coward. That fact alone is all that allows me to close my eyes at night.

The sadness at my life is nowhere near the angst that the Jews endured in World War II. I'm upset over. I'm upset over how my life has been going, but no one broke my body. Someone took advantage of it, hurt it, tried to tear it apart, but they didn't break it. The bodies of the Jews were, the thousands upon thousands who were brutally murdered because of their own heritage; people who did nothing to deserve their graves. Yet, they were forced to dig trenches and be shot to fall down in them. That goes beyond my mind's comprehension. How can I know pain?

I don't undermine my grief, or that of anyone else. I can't imagine, though, any situation worse than being a Jew in the 1940s. But there were those who survived and are still alive today. My scars put next to theirs are pathetic. The memories those survivors have must be terrible to live with, but they still wake up each morning and live. Where do I find that strength? Do I already have it? I couldn't even begin to imagine... What if I was forced to watch my son burn in a blazing fire? What if we were both at the mercy of cruel and perverted guards? How would I keep us both alive? How would I even find the strength to live at will? I've been given such a small task.

Who it happened with is not nearly as important as what happened. It's what happened that I never want to forget. My hate for him will only grow, and that hate will manifest itself in the most self-destructive ways possible. I can't let him win. I gave up fighting once before, but I won't give in again. I won't die.

"What all these victims need above all is to know that they are not alone; that we are not forgetting them, that when their voices are stifled, we shall lend them ours; that while their freedom depends on ours, the quality of our freedom depends on theirs." I have faith that, someday, I won't be afraid to speak anymore. But until that day comes, I will lend my pen to the silenced, and write the words we're all afraid to say.

Diary, I'm going to write my story. I don't want to have anymore secrets. Withholding the truth will only rob someone else the chance to say, "I thought I was the only one." Secrets aren't nearly as effective as exposure of the truth. And I need to do this, for me. I want someone to read the words I can't say. A good way to start might be to get those words out on paper.

Jessie

Monday, May 25, 2009
Dear Diary,
  We've had graduation practice all day, and it's been horrible. I didn't want to walk, didn't have a gown, and I told all of my teachers that I wasn't going to walk. Mrs. Tamson came to the school not long after that, and to say she wasn't happy about that is a huge understatement. She called me by my full name, which she has never done before. She said, "You're walking if I have to force you into a gown and push you on the stage!" So... I guess I'm walking. I don't have a gown, but I'll find one. One of the teachers in charge of graduation said that they had extra from previous years.
  Before, I didn't want to walk because I didn't want a million eyes on me, nor did I want to draw attention to myself. Now that I've gone through with a rehearsal, I can see that the people on the last row with me aren't... the brightest crayons in the box, so to speak. They're making stupid jokes the whole time, being loud, and making fun of everyone on stage. My blood boiled when they called Mr. Jones something really foul, and I felt horrible when I didn't stand up for him. My dad isn't going to be there for graduation night, most likely, so I'd be walking for myself. But I don't think I would be considered selfish if I did myself the favor of participating that night for myself.
                    Jessie

Tuesday, May 26, 2009
Dear Diary,
  Brice got into Governors School! He got a call that

Where My Ink Comes From

whoever he was alternate for dropped out of the program, and there was an opening if he wanted it. I'm so happy for him! I know he's going to have fun there, and maybe when he gets out of Green County, he can see where his talent can truly take him. Congratulations, Brice...

Jessie

Thursday, May 28, 2009
Dear Diary,

    Senior night was tonight. All the seniors were honored by having their names called out along with their school activities and accomplishments. My dad didn't want to go, but it didn't even matter anymore. I wanted to go for me. I wanted to hear the senior English teacher call my name and read off all the things I had done – Marching Band, Pep Band, Concert Band, poetry publications, bound for Murray State University – because it was just a reminder that I'm almost there. So what if tonight was for the parents? I did something for me for once. Moms matter too, right?

    And Diary, I am going to Murray. As scared as I am of how things will be there, one thought scares me even more. More than the thought of what will happen if I go... what will happen if I don't?

Jessie

Friday, May 29, 2009
Dear Diary,

    Last page again. It's ironic that it would fall on

graduation night.

I'm sorry that you won't get to see me go to Murray State. It's not like my journals typically get a goodbye, because I just carry the story over without making the transition obvious. But you have a black leather cover with a lace bookmark that I loved.

As I'm writing, I'm watching the tears and the smiles on the faces of everyone I've grown up with, hated, and loved. Benjamin is sitting next to me in his carrier asleep. Something people rarely get to see; a single high school mother in a graduate's attire. Benjamin should be so proud...

I've waited a long time for the day I could say this. I never thought I would get to say it, but thank God I finally can: I survived. I survived. To Benjamin, Daniel, Brice, Jamie, Melanie, Marissa, Mandy, Jones, Tamson, Riley, Jordan, Brooke, Lauren, Mary, every son-of-a-bitch who said I couldn't do it, and every angel who said I could, I survived. Despite the horrible circumstances, despite the things I've seen and done, and what I've been through, despite all the people and the statistics that told me I was a failure and that I wouldn't make it, I survived. To Benjamin's father who tried to break me, to the brother who hates me, to the family who wanted me to give up, to the naysayers who wanted to hurt me with their words, I survived.

I do have to say... you probably carried me farther than any other journal has. You were there in my life's darkest year, and on the longest nights, when no one else was. Thanks for getting me through it. It looks like my pen was stronger than the circumstances, stronger than the world, and it prevailed. I've won. I survived. My pen is fueled by the words of wonderful teachers, the encouragement of wonderful friends, the pain of a past that still stings, and the hands that came too close for me to forget. My past is all that will ensure my words later on, and I will never forget from where my ink comes from.

Speaking of my pen... I've been contemplating how to

best go about this book idea. And I think I've figured it out. Diary, somewhere in your pages, I've left my heart. I'll never be this honest again, not to anyone else, and I think it's time I let the world read the words I've written and left there. You are my story. And I think I know exactly how I want you to begin…

Sunday, January 13, 2008
    Dear Diary,
    I love the smell of new paper in a journal. I go through one faster than I go through Wal*Mart sweaters…

Epilogue

American artist Norman Rockwell once wrote, "The view of life I communicate in my pictures excludes the sordid and ugly. I paint life as I would like it to be." I think, at least in some small way, we are all like Rockwell in that we paint our worlds as we want them to be.

There are two types of people in the world: those who paint the picture and those who pose for the painting. Some commentate on the story, while others star as the characters. Despite what type of person you are, it's in everyone's most basic core human desire to leave behind a mark that warrants remembrance. But sometimes during our strive for greatness, we lose ourselves in the process. And sometimes it takes a little magic to bring us back. But, we don't always have to look in novels like Harry Potter or Lord of the Rings to find something mystical. It can often be found in simplicity: In the bars of a song, a baby's laugh, the delicate strength of a spider's web, the composition of a leaf, or in the eyes of someone we love.

Sometimes it's in others that we find ourselves. I once had a teacher whose first assignment was to explain to her who I was; and at the time, I only thought I knew who that person was looking back at me through the mirror. It wasn't until much later that I discovered that you can't truly describe a person, not to any accuracy, anyway. A person is more than ink on a page or the mere description of words. They are more than the car they drove or the clothes they once wore. And we are all given an entire lifetime to do with what we wish, contorting, applying, and taking away anything we desire.

But all of life is but a coming home, a journey to travel, a question not to be answered but instead to be lived. During the trek from birth to death we are changed by certain individuals whose destiny far surpasses even themselves. We are, on occasion, blessed by something Heaven-sent, something larger than the realms of reality. And through those influences, we are molded into the people who we were meant to become. It's not always an attractive or glamorous venture, but it's one we all must take. It often requires courage and vigilance, but even still we sometimes fall into the darkness. But falling down is simply part of life, albeit a small one, a tribulation through which we must all walk. For it is only in the moments that we trip, stumble, and crash to the ground that we learn to pick ourselves up. And as we begin to stand back on solid ground with bloody knees and dirt on our faces, we can look back at the place from which we came and know that this is it; this is the person who we were meant to become, painting our world the way we wish with a little magic.

--Derrick C. Ford

About the Author

C.N. King was born and raised in Birdsville, Kentucky. She began a serious writing career at the age of 16 after attending the Young Adult Theatre Academy at the Riverpark Center in Owensboro. She started out writing short stories, but promises that her true passion will always lie with songwriting. King is a mother, now currently enrolled at Murray State University, where she is pursuing a degree in music education. She hopes to one day go back to the high school from which she graduated from - Livingston Central High School - and inspire others to express themselves in the arts, be it the instrument or the pen.

Some of King's hobbies and interests include music, playing guitar and piano, reading, computers, live theatre, art, movies, psychology, and photography. She has written two other unpublished books, which she hopes to have published in the near future. Her goal is to use the trials of her life to inspire others to survive their own.

King may be contacted at cn.king@ymail.com

Epilogue

American artist Norman Rockwell once wrote, "The view of life I communicate in my pictures excludes the sordid and ugly. I paint life as I would like it to be." I think, at least in some small way, we are all like Rockwell in that we paint our worlds as we want them to be.

There are two types of people in the world: those who paint the picture and those who pose for the painting. Some commentate on the story, while others star as the characters. Despite what type of person you are, it's in everyone's most basic core human desire to leave behind a mark that warrants remembrance. But sometimes during our strive for greatness, we lose ourselves in the process. And sometimes it takes a little magic to bring us back. But, we don't always have to look in novels like Harry Potter or Lord of the Rings to find something mystical. It can often be found in simplicity: In the bars of a song, a baby's laugh, the delicate strength of a spider's web, the composition of a leaf, or in the eyes of someone we love.

Sometimes it's in others that we find ourselves. I once had a teacher whose first assignment was to explain to her who I was; and at the time, I only thought I knew who that person was looking back at me through the mirror. It wasn't until much later that I discovered that you can't truly describe a person, not to any accuracy, anyway. A person is more than ink on a page or the mere description of words. They are more than the car they drove or the clothes they once wore. And we are all given an entire lifetime to do with what we wish, contorting, applying, and taking away anything we desire.

But all of life is but a coming home, a journey to travel,

a question not to be answered but instead to be lived. During the trek from birth to death we are changed by certain individuals whose destiny far surpasses even themselves. We are, on occasion, blessed by something Heaven-sent, something larger than the realms of reality. And through those influences, we are molded into the people who we were meant to become. It's not always an attractive or glamorous venture, but it's one we all must take. It often requires courage and vigilance, but even still we sometimes fall into the darkness. But falling down is simply part of life, albeit a small one, a tribulation through which we must all walk. For it is only in the moments that we trip, stubble, and crash to the ground that we learn to pick ourselves up. And as we begin to stand back on solid ground with bloody knees and dirt on our faces, we can look back at the place from which we came and know that this is it; this is the person who we were meant to become, painting our world the way we wish with a little magic.

--Derrick C. Ford
"A believer in magic"

About the Author

C.N. King was born and raised in Birdsville, Kentucky. She began a serious writing career at the age of 16 after attending the Young Adult Theatre Academy at the Riverpark Center in Owensboro. She started out writing short stories, but promises that her true passion will always lie with songwriting. King is a mother, now currently enrolled at Murray State University, where she is pursuing a degree in music education. She hopes to one day return to Livingston Central High School from which she graduated and inspire others to express themselves in the arts, be it the instrument or the pen.

Some of King's hobbies and interests include music, playing guitar and piano, reading, computers, live theatre, art, movies, psychology, and photography. She has written two other unpublished books, which she hopes to have published in the near future. Her goal is to use the trials of her life to inspire others to survive their own.

King may be contacted at *cn.king@ymail.com*

Made in the USA